# American Treasure

# American Treasure

## JILL MCDONOUGH

Alice James Books
New Gloucester, Maine
www.alicejamesbooks.org

10 9 8 7 6 5 4 3 2 1

Alice James Books are published by Alice James Poetry Cooperative, Inc.

Alice James Books
Auburn Hall
60 Pineland Drive, Suite 206
New Gloucester, ME 04260
www.alicejamesbooks.org

Library of Congress Cataloging-in-Publication Data

Names: McDonough, Jill, author.
Title: American treasure / Jill McDonough.
Description: New Gloucester, ME : Alice James Books, [2022]
Identifiers: LCCN 2022024210 (print) | LCCN 2022024211 (ebook) | ISBN
    9781948579292 (trade paperback) | ISBN 9781948579384 (epub)
Subjects: LCGFT: Poetry.
Classification: LCC PS3613.C3885 A82 2022  (print) | LCC PS3613.C3885
    (ebook) | DDC 811/.6--dc23/eng/20220524
LC record available at https://lccn.loc.gov/2022024210
LC ebook record available at https://lccn.loc.gov/2022024211

Alice James Books gratefully acknowledges support from individual donors, private foundations, the National
Endowment for the Arts, and the Amazon Literary Partnership. Funded in part by a grant from the Maine Arts
Commission, an independent state agency supported by the National Endowment for the Arts.

Cover art: Photograph by Susan Mikula

# Contents

## One

# Two

# Three

# ONE

# Zero Slave Teeth

On the radio I hear about George Washington's teeth.
A guest says *what do you think his teeth were* and a host
says *wood*. I've read about Waterloo teeth, how we prowled
battlefields, plucked teeth from young French corpses,
wired them into fresh rich people mouths.
I figure we're about to learn the founding father's teeth
were from his soldiers. But it's worse than that: slave teeth.
I post this on Facebook, asking what might the reparations
be for having your teeth pulled, having to see your teeth
every day in your owner's stupid mouth. Melodie posts a comic
from *The Oatmeal*: this is old news, the slave teeth thing, also
that people LOSE THEIR MINDS denying it. She posts
the comic and we watch the losing of minds unfold.
*He had a wooden tooth (teeth). . . zero slave teeth,*
some stranger says, calls me a *stupid cunt* on my dad's page.
My DAD. Zero slave teeth. No innocents on death row. No
lynchings, not all men. Everybody crying rape, not all slave
owners were bad. Sally Hemings? In love. Three hots
and a cot. Must be nice! FREEDOM FREEDOM USA!

# Sonnet for Reading Aloud in Kidjail

The boys in my local juvie want to work one
on one, write stories, poems, mark up the stuff
I give them. More than one kid at a time's less fun:
more fussing, more holding back to show how tough
they are. When one of them writes on the other's paper
the germophobic one loses his shit; I get it, sit
between them while they write their poems. Later
I read them aloud so they can hear how good they are; it's
like a magic trick, their words in my grown-up voice.
They still and listen, hear themselves, lean in on me
like children, because they are children. Two boys,
one on either side, a slow relax from anger in to breathe.
Their warm weights, cool of classroom, fresh pencils, stacks
of paper. Me feeling them thinking *That sounds pretty good. Dag.*

# Our Star

"It's from *The Daily Galaxy*."
—Susan Mikula

I tell Susan about walking around the Templo Mayor,
the pyramid in the middle of Mexico City. The gutter
for the sewer pipe they dug, a straight shot through
the ruins, 1905. How they must have been so over
all of it, the skull-shaped stones just another thing
to roll your eyes at, chuck out of your weary way.
Toss the fucking stone skulls on the rubble heap
with the feathered mantles, jaguar bones, python
skins, real skulls. I describe all this for Susan while
we wait in the waiting room for her dog, beloved Poppy,
who's stashed somewhere getting chemo, and we talk
about how time works. Out the window the Roosevelt
Island tram slips back and forth along its wire.
Susan tells me when they tried to dig a parking garage
below LACMA, they unearthed a woolly mammoth stuck
in the tar pits, *where the earth bubbles up to the top*,
she says, so over all of that. She loves woolly mammoths
like she loves the Weimar Republic, googles "ice baby"
to find the third result, after Vanilla Ice, some ice-
cream truck: a baby woolly mammoth left behind

for us to find and look at on her phone between
Stichelton soup recipes and them giving us back
our damn dog. We read from *The Daily Galaxy*
on coronal holes, which *spew streams of high-speed
solar wind*. Oh, our star! We make a note to look up
the Carrington Event, learn someday how solar winds
can corrode pipes, disrupt even Susan's Candy Crush.

# Missile and Space Gallery, National Museum of the U.S. Air Force

All we want is to look all day at drones, the Kettering Bug
and Firebee, the hangar full of once-secret aircraft,
now decades old, still looking like our dystopian future, yours.
Also the rifle that shot the first shot from an airplane,
August 20, 1910, less than seven years since man first flew.
*The next month Fickel and Curtiss repeated the experiment*
*using an Army semi-automatic pistol.* We find blunder trophies.
Practice, atomic, and cluster bombs. Operation Carpetbagger.
Black Widow, Grasshopper, Hoverfly. We almost skipped
the Missile Gallery, tucked off to one side. When we walked in
we stepped into an enchanted circle of missiles, decommissioned
missiles pouring up like a redwood grove. Two Minutemans,
a Jupiter, Thors and Titans. A Peacekeeper, its naming-of-parts
poster topped with a faux-funky font: *PEACEKEEPER*!

The radar off Provincetown looks for ICBMs like this one,
new and improved versions of this one. The radar looks
for the end of the world, so we can make it worse. End
more. End harder. Yes, of course, deterrence, but still.
Everyone who walks into the Missile and Space Gallery,
its 140-foot silo, looks up and just says *wow*. Everyone.

When we did it we heard laughter, looked up to see people
who'd done the same thing. We took the glass elevator up
to the balcony to watch for more, watch the door, laugh
when we saw it again and again: *wow* and *wow*, then *wow*.

# Joe Hill's Prison

The Historical Society in Salt Lake still has
some letters, a pamphlet called "Joe Hill's
Remains," even though he made it clear
he wanted his ashes scattered in every state
except Utah. Not wanting to be caught dead
here. The prison where Joe Hill died
is torn down now. Now there's a Sizzler. Neon
and brick at the foot of mountains he must
have looked at through bars. They're beautiful
mountains. They look like America, all majesty.
Rising purple up beyond the wall where he was shot.

# Alone in Utah

I go out to eat because I'm lonely.
The waitresses are lovely. I tip well.
I spread my papers out, eat in the kind
of places that have booths, scalloped
paper place mats, line drawings of presidents.
Nixon looks like Bush. Everyone kind
and funny, students writing their brave
hearts out even when the power fails
and I have them write in deepening
gloaming, snow soft on the windows, turning
white to gray in the ambient light.
One girl writes about her stint in the loony
bin, *the broken feeling*, feeling broken
then, some better now. She writes about hallways
and we see them, footsteps, dirty socks and I say
*we have to find a way to get out from under*
*the bed*. We laugh and laugh. It's
a wonderful class, and I wished I was dead.

What a thing to say. But it took me all day
to get out of bed that winter. It's chemical,
the distance from Josey a kind of radiation,
homesick in my body, nausea. This is how

to do it: crawl out of bed, bent double with cramps,
weep on the toilet, go on. A cup of coffee, water
boiled for tea. Trick yourself into moving
with promises: a drink after work, a movie.
*so-not-into-it-dot-com*, I'd think, hauling myself
over to the classroom, charging myself: three
hours. Give them what they deserve.
Waiting tables, I chose to love the ones
I poured coffee for. Now I let myself fill
with tenderness for undergrads and murderers,
imagine them as children, little boys and girls.
Privilege and wonder, her underbite and glasses.
His new haircut, her white socks.

# What We Can Imagine

"It has been worse than anything you can imagine."
—Kathleen DeSerio, plaintiff in *DeSerio v. Ingraham*, on her neighbor's
baseball diamond

She can't see the photo, quote will stand in Sunday's
*New York Times* beside the war crimes, famine, hurricanes.
So much is worse than this lush land above a ball field.

Her belfried house above despised green velvet, perfect
pats of white the bases, home. Working men working
on smooth infield, outfield. They wave.

The zoning: bleachers are out. Also aluminum bats.
*It has been worse than anything you can imagine.*
Worse than stained machetes, rivers full of bloated cows.

Worse being hungry, getting stabbed or getting
fired. Bear with me, now, Kathleen: the sound of far-off
cheering, the smack of wooden bat to ball, that's worse

than, say, someone breaking in and knifing all your chairs? Worse
than never knowing love? The imagination reels: the people stand in line
to trade their lot with yours. The *Times* includes a photo. Standing stiff

and pained, your arms are folded, lips thin. Tight. Your place
is thick with trees. Beyond them you can see, in miniature,
the ball field. It has been worse than anything you can imagine.

Worst thing there is in Tewksbury—in the full soul, collective
imagination of New Jersey, nothing's worse. Kathleen DeSerio
is serious. She means it; read those lips. Her villain,

Mr. Ingraham, says, appealingly, God-damned-Americanly,
*If they try to stop us they're going to have to drag me off*
*that field in handcuffs.* His photo, taken late some sunny afternoon:

the shadows of a boy, his father, long beside their gloved and batted
bodies. Armed against the weak imagination of DeSerio.
The field wide behind them, glorious and mowed.

# College Reading and Writing in Grown-up Jail

I tell a student his handwriting looks like beautiful grafitti and he says, a little proud, surprised I noticed, *that was my first adult sentence!*

On the day I hand out fresh notebooks two of the women, one after the other, walk in the room, see the notebooks, and say *CAN I HAVE TWO?* I crack up, point out they are the only ones who asked and the only white people in the class. I write *white privilege* on the board, talk about how it works, white people expecting twice as much. They laugh, we all laugh, and when I am packing up to leave, walk out the doors, they call out *white privilege!* and I say *you're not wrong!*

One of the white women liked my boots and suggested we trade. The students all wear white sneakers. I said *Excellent plan! No one will ever notice you are wearing hot pink suede Uggs bedazzled with crystal crowns.* I asked the students what they can *INFER* about me because of those boots, pointing out they are already keen analysts, they just need to apply those skills to the text. This makes them happy. This and my ridiculous boots.

I hear some of the things they did and look at Flint, Puerto Rico, kids in cages, think this government makes even their violent crimes look like shoplifting. You can only hurt so many people at a time with your one body. And usually it's yours getting hurt.

I hear one of the students tell another teacher about a problem with her medication, and he tells her *You're incarcerated but you still have constitutional rights.* She smirks, says *WHERE THEY AT?*

One woman in orange ICE scrubs only speaks Romanian, can't read or write in English. I write the alphabet for her, teach her how to write *MY NAME IS* and ask what else she wants to learn to write. She wants to write *I MISS MY CHILDREN,* so I teach her, help her write their names and ages, names she touches after she writes, with little finger pats.

# Big Earth

Outside the Buffalo stadium before the Pats-
Bills game, a C-130 dips down to say *GO BILLS*.
A Buffalo fan tells us the National Guard
practices touch-and-goes for hours, the move
they use to drop supplies. Slip down so close,
pop open the hatch, strap a chute to the goods, pull up,
and parachuted pallets zip out the back.
I say *Like the Berlin Airlift,* Operation
Little Vittles, how *Onkel Wackelflügel*—
Uncle Wiggly Wings—cut loose
candy rations, floating Hershey bars. This
is the right thing to say. The Bills fan, Mike,
likes this, loved to fly in the war. *Only thing
better than flying was killing people*, he laughs.
He pantomimes picking the enemy out of trees
from above. I tell him I once flew over a herd
of red deer, saw it split and spill like water. These
are my people, these Pats and Bills fans, shrugging over
concussions 'cause what can you do? He says when he
was a kid he couldn't wait to kill bad guys,
but now he's not convinced they're all so bad.
He points to the Pats fans, Bills fans yukking it up
across the street, giving each other a ration

of shit, but grinning, keeping it light. *Right,* I say. *Choose your enemies. There's room for everybody.*

Mike nods. *That's right. It's a big earth.*

# Lucky Ladies Sestina

for Josey, on her 50th birthday

I wake up with you, warm in the dark blankets, safe
our whole lives but still sort of surprised. Lucky ladies,
living together, up in our own damn house. No sick babies,
no hunger, getting yelled at, getting hit. We get to be alive now,
rescued by here, by us. Some equity, our plenty of time. Back then
my grandma's mom got given away, parents too poor
to keep her. My grandfather lived in a Masonic Home for Poor
Widows and Orphans, dropped off by his dad when an unsafe
abortion killed their mom. They never knew. Back then
button hooks, bleeding out in bathtubs: the family's ladies
knew all about it, but nobody told the men. For now
nobody dies. Here. Because of that. But plenty of babies
go unwanted, and whole families leave Syria, bring babies
we seem to think are proto-terrorists. Humans! Poor
humans, so sure we deserve everything we have now.
Plus more. Sure everything's earned, nothing sacrificed to be safe
as houses here. I like to think of the ships and tenements, loony bins, ladies
hating staying home but doing it, saddled with proto-us. And then
think of our problems: the oil bill, AAA, overdraft charges, UPS. Back then
we'd probably be whores, or witches, all our rape-babies
born to die young. We read about corpse meditation, meet ladies
for lunch in museums, choose new wines. I meditate on prison, the poor
prisoners, fluorescent quiver of those classrooms, their chill. Safe

to say I'm spoiled. A car! A dishwasher! A dryer! We hustled. Now
we hunker down. You know every decent bartender in town now;
most of them you trained your sweet self, your swole knees. Back then
I taught seven classes, you pulled shifts through pneumonia, only safe
with that money coming in. I teach *deeds* dancing in a *green bay,* bees
being *buccaneers of buzz,* make Sestina Worksheets for my poor
students: hungry grad students, undergrads working four jobs, ladies
on probation in the Southie Court House, cafeterias full of ladies
still in jail. Even they, alive today, can't understand me now,
how I was confused when a guard yelled at me, explained to the poor
ladies *Nobody tells me what to do.* They were stunned, said *Dag,* then
we got back to work. Their essays on Desdemona, Lady MacBeth's babies.
You and I decide what we want for dinner: someplace new or something safe,
a Caesar salad, roast chicken. Ladies love chicken, a glass of red wine. Then
we nestle down with our books, silken sleep. Now we sleep like babies,
safe as houses, for all those poor babies before us, who never got to be safe.

# In Praise of Black Boys on Motorbikes in Boston

Because they are fearless, show everyone their joy and strength.
Because in so many other moments we take their lives.

Because it makes me happy to see their flock swoop past me on the street.
Because we lock them up.

Because I see more black boys and black men locked up than on campus.
Because once I heard a man say *I took a shortcut once. It cost me two years.*

Because we so rarely see the pursuit of happiness, the moment of its
  attainment.
Because their balance is youth in action, strength and grace.

They stand on their bike seats, or kneel and weave.
I smile and gawk when I hear them coming.

Because I get starstruck.
Because I remember the verb for wheelies is "to pop."

Because spotting them is like seeing a famous person, or Keytar Bear.
Because we can see their happiness better with no helmet.

I catch my breath, breathe *Oh Honey Be Careful* to myself.
When I see them I smile and wave so they know I love them.

Because once I caught up to a group at a red light
after watching them run so many red lights,

and the one closest to me was on one knee, no helmet.
I managed not to say *Oh Honey Be Careful.*

Instead I said *I think you are amazing and I hope you live forever.*
And he said *Thank you. You, too.*

# Crying in the Cab Away from You

Right now it's a music video for some urban version
of a sad country song, my life, with swelling strings—or, really,
they're twanging chords. Susan's dear hand raised, small
and getting smaller through the raindrop-spotted rear
window of the cab. Then she picks her way across the puddled
street, while I look out the window I roll down. My made-up film
reflects Eighth Ave.'s storefronts and people in my eyes, the sweet
dumb tears on my cheek, before I wipe them quick with the back
of one dry hand. Sometimes I get to go visit my best friends, forget
my phone charger, earrings, then head home with their charger
coiled careful in the rubber band Rachel's hands organized
around it, new gold hoop earrings from Susan I'll never take out.
In the cab, a Bergdorf Goodman bag of homemade curry supper
and lemon cookies on my lap, I go ahead and cry some: what the hell.
I'm so in love with my friends and life, my marriage, yours, New York,
the whole place looking like a Richard Scarry children's book, maybe
*Busy, Busy World* or *What Do People Do All Day?* I love the man
singing along with his headphones, wagging his big head and a finger
at whoever done him wrong. Well-dressed women waiting for a walk
light. The GNCs and pink sex shops, dive bars and chain drugstores.
This driver doesn't notice that I'm crying, or he pretends, leaves me
alone. But I remember another one, some other time I cried, so
sad to leave you guys—was I moving across the country? Headed back

to that Utah job? That sad apartment, its pleather couch and popcorn
ceilings, Jiffy Pop suppers I ate alone. That driver saw, said *Aw!*
*You miss your friend!* He'd seen Susan hail his cab and hug me,
hand me my bags. And he said *Don't cry; you'll see your friend again.*
But even now, years later, writing it down, *you'll see your friend again*
makes me tear up. You don't know that, Mr. Cab Man! Not one of us
knows anything at all. All we can do is have a good time when we're
together, cry a little when we're apart. While the smokestacks, skyline,
East River all get smaller. While everyone gets further away from now.

# Sestina for the Women Locked Up at Framingham, Who Make American Flags

For years I'd drive out there to see the women
in College Writing, Af Am History, Memoir. I'd walk past flags
for the Commonwealth of Massachusetts, P.O.W.s, America, make
them write essays on Nabokov, Dumpster diving, American
foreign policy. Hiroshima, Hannah Arendt, Shakespeare. C.O.s blocked
my way in for random rules: some weeks I could wear my hair up,
some weeks I could not wear my hair up.
We'd read *Othello*, annotate the text; I taught them to flag
every line about racism, every line about love. Evidence to lock
down an arguable thesis. Sometimes I could make the women
laugh, sometimes they were too depressed. Their American
History was spotty; they joked they were too high in high school to take
it seriously. So Hannah Arendt time meant I had to make
them understand the Holocaust. Explain it just quick, before time's up.
Most of what they knew of Nazis was *Hogan's Heroes*, Colonel Klink.
    Oh, America.
I begged them to look it up in the library when I was gone. Swastika flags
and concentration camps, gas chambers, shaving women's
heads, everybody in striped uniforms transported and locked
up together: some awkward parallels. Which reminds me: I lucked
into tickets for a tour of Mount Vernon, could see where George
    Washington made
his enslaved workers sleep on crowded bunks. An old woman

on the tour said *it looks like Auschwitz*. My friend LaShaun smiled up
sweetly, said *No. Auschwitz looks like this*. It's true; American flags,
up over prisons, slave quarters, internment camps. American
history: so embarrassing. Good thing everything's better now! American
prison industries like MassCor make so many things with locked-
up labor: maybe paying pennies a day should be a red flag?
What, I want them to laze around or carve shivs instead of make
things? No new skills, no sewn stripes or embroidered stars? Shut up.
It's just crazy that they make these particular things. The men
in New Hampshire make LIVE FREE OR DIE license plates; women
at Framingham learn digital embroidery, make all the American
flags. What if we paid them fairly? Or just their families? It's fucked up
to make money off people in prison, right? Scarlett O'Hara leasing men
    locked
to a mill was on her, and it's against the law for states to sell what
    inmates make
across state lines. So we know it's wrong. But I bought one of the flags,
put it up outside my house beside the rainbow flags, Black
Lives Matter banners of my neighborhood. Two women in America
on a safe block, our car in our driveway, all the freedom that we make.

# A Decision Was Made

*A decision was made to fire a Hellfire missile.*
*It was fired,* Donald Rumsfeld said with his mouth,

his breath, on purpose, what he wants us to hear. We hear
what he does not want us to hear. The unknown unknowns,

the known et cetera. The missile was made, was named,
was fired. The women were raped, the people enslaved.

Blacks were slaves, I learned in school—French Broad Elementary,
the halls carpeted, the poor janitor always coming around

with some kind of powder to soak up the vomit, little kids always
getting sick. Why'd they do that? Who'd consent to such

a crappy life? No one taught me white people enslaved black ones.
I learned rape prevention: take a whistle, don't dress like a whore.

Not *don't rape anybody.* Thanks, syntax. We don't know who's
on our kill lists not because they're secret, or only in part; also

because nobody knows. The Guy in the White Truck Who Drives
Out to That Compound on Tuesdays, say. The Man Who Kicks the Goats.

*Indicators were there that there was something untoward*
*that we needed to make go away*, Pentagon spokeman Stufflebeem said.

Stufflebeam's the kind of guy who'll tell a girl he's a widower to get
in her pants. Breast cancer. Damn shame. Nice country

you got here. Shame if anything happened to it. *Make it disappear,*
we tell people about our problems. *Make it go away. I want him gone.*

# Dante Accidentally Kicks a Face: Jefferson, Nixon, Trump

In Robert Rauschenberg's *Inferno*, Virgil and Dante
walk through the ninth circle, hell-heads frozen in place
like asshole mushrooms. They are traitors to country.
Stepping around them, Dante "accidentally kicks a face."

Accidentally, my ass. I get it: all we need is one to squeal,
flip, whatever. One loose-lipped bastard ice-fast next to him:
next thing you know they're spilling everything. They roll
on all their fellow traitors, whole White House full of them,

a Manafort of dominoes. All of us thinking *treason*
these days, *traitor* on every-pussy-body's lips. Lie
down with dogs, losers: we're done with collusion,
mere meddling, obstruction. An eye for an eye,

bitches; no honor among thieves. We watched you make
your nasty presidential beds. Everybody knows
better! Everybody knows you don't sell out your country, make
slaves of your own kids. Don't puff up all proud, come home

stoked to lose a million lives and peace in Viet Nam
to get yourself elected. You guys suck. One swift kick and we've
got everybody, what shit-for-brains they haven't gnawed
on yet, *who betrayed his people for money.*

*As soon as a soul commits betrayal…a devil*
*displaces it, governs inside the body:* these traitors
still here don't even know they're dead. *Who are still*
*here, still eat and drink and sleep* looking *still alive on earth.*

# Heirloom

*The New York Times* reveals a man has bought,
at auction, a forty-five-hundred dollar mummified
hand. *Hopefully it doesn't have any bad*
*seeds attached* he said, the sort of line
that should be followed with "he quipped." We know
what he almost means: a curse, a vengeful mummy,
rest disturbed, his corpse exhumed, his hand—
long ivory nails, frayed linen, delicate bones
in a tannic sort-of leather—broken off,
and sold at auction. The hand-buyer intends
it as an heirloom for his kids. Across
the country, warm toast in our mouths, we shake
our heads, turn to our spouses, smack the paper and say
*It's a goddamn mummy's hand, you stupid fuck,*
as if the hand bestowed its owner with
the power to hear collective common sense.
The Monkey's Paw, The Hand of Glory, now in New York
it drums its fingers, biding its endless time.

# Sally Hemings and Kitty Genovese

We are watching a documentary about Kitty Genovese, stabbed
in front of silent witnesses in Queens. Turns out the story's
very different from the one we know. So what's new, right?

At first it seems like she got stabbed for no reason.
I'm confused, ask Josey *What's the point*
*of stabbing someone if you're not going to rape them?*
We laugh; we are cynical, shrugging on a sofa. If
*why didn't he rape her?* is a logical question, what kind
of world are we living in? Wait, I know! It's ours!

Anyway, turns out he *did* rape her. So the world
we grew up in makes sense again to us.

We keep talking to men about Sally Hemings. Men keep
using the word *concubine*, and we talk about what counts
as consent. One of them finally helps us sound this out, joking
*Sure, but what's the point of having slaves if you aren't going*
*to have sex with them?* We are startled by the clear
and sudden light of the best defense of slavery we have
ever heard. Maps of the agrarian south, Eli Whitney, cane
and bales of cotton, States' Rights: they all pale
compared to this. We are all more right than we have any right

to know. When they catch Kitty's killer they ask what he was up to that night: *Finding a woman and killing her*, he says. The police ask, reasonably, *And raping her?*

And Kitty's killer answers, shrugging: *Possibly*.

# Introductory Composition at a Massachusetts Prison

Jason and Cy and Bobby write
about arrogance, power, how it makes you
blind. Jimmy and Dougie are dealing with exile,
who gives it, who takes it away. *I am no honest man,*
Edmund says, *I have told you what I have seen*
*and heard;—but faintly—*. A silk-screened Malcom
X, stacks of folding chairs on cabinets, chipped
silver paint on rusting radiators. Matt and Butch talk
bad fathers, hurt and disappointed girls. Luis
and Jim are all about Cordelia; revolutionary,
or just immature? The others are all over Lear:
Lear victimizes his loved ones, Lear's delusion of control.
Lear's madness healed by depression, by which we think
he means humility. High-gloss cream on concrete blocks,
chalkboards, not enough chalk. Lurid unfurled map
of these United States. I will punish home, says Lear, and
we whisper what it is to punish, what we mean by home.

Two

# Freedom

I talk to the students in jail about freedom, how in America
we obsess over it, write it over flags on T-shirts, spread

it around under eagles. It has something to do with guns
and fireworks, Harley-Davidsons, New Hampshire, living free

until you're dead. I tell the students I think the people
fetishizing freedom don't mean it. They really mean

LOOK OVER HERE, AWAY FROM ALL THE SLAVERY
WE DID, AWAY FROM ALL THE JAIL! I tell them they

are the experts, ask them to write what freedom means:
*privacy is freedom and if you feel held back, afraid*

*to do something, you're not completely free.    No fear*
*of loss, no fear of hunger, no fear of pain.    A body*

*to call my own, a voice driven by my own mind.*
*The security of a dry, warm place to sleep.    To own*

*my own time left here.    Being able to hold my son*
*at night.    Showering in private.    Freedom to me*

*is having the choice to walk away from a fight.* Freedom
a work in progress. Everyday freedom, the real work for us all.

# I Ain't Afraid of Nothing about This Test

When the box of books comes to the house, plastic-wrapped
stacks of a book I wrote, I take one into the juvie, show it
to the boys I work with, use it for reading comprehension.
This is a good idea. *It's FIFTEEN DOLLARS!* they holler.
They want to know how much money I make from selling
my books, tell me where they would sell them, where I could
take them to sell. They see the author photo, get so excited
they crack me up: *Miss, that's you!* One wants to know *Does
it have a gold sticker on it?* Not yet. I read them a poem called
"Afraid," then ask them what I'm afraid of, what I do to be brave.
They do great, write their own poems about what they're afraid of.
One can't think of anything that scares him, he's so brave.
I ask what he's afraid of about taking the HiSET again,
the high school equivalency exam he keeps failing. *I ain't afraid
of nothing about this test,* he says, and I say Great! That's the title
of your poem: now just write a list of all the things you'd
be afraid of if you *were* afraid. *Is it a list or a poem?* Both.
The list will be the poem. The list of things he's not afraid of
is long. Not afraid of losing focus, not afraid of being wrong.

# The Serious Downer

I tell Josey when she dies I am going to eat her face
before I call the cops. They'll be on their way

to pick up her dead body and I won't be able to stop, finally able
to bite adorable chunks of her perfect cheeks, gnaw on the regal

cleft of that much-beloved chin. I am always already hot
to chew on Josey somehow: the side of her hand, the part

you press to frosted or fogged-up glass to make a little
baby's foot; one rough knuckle plucked up in the middle

of the day at a red light, her cool hand on the stick.
I tell her the EMTs for the dead, the morgue guys, will walk

in on me, her blood by now darkening and crusting
all over my mouth, me looking up like *dag, busted,*

mouth agape and also full of one last bite of her unchewed body.
*But it'll be so sad; you won't be there to think it's funny,*

I say. *That would be the drag,* adds Josey, nodding, complacent.
*That would be the serious downer of that situation.*

# Backhoe in Snow, Boston

When the backhoe got stuck in the snow on our street,
another backhoe came to help. Then the little buddy backhoe
got stuck, too. Traffic piling up behind them, a mail truck,
ten cars. Nobody honks: too tired. *What're you gonna do?*
the drivers shrug. The snow falls, still falling, an always
already of snow in the rising dark. Our mailman, our hero,
helps push, everybody shoveling, doing their part, until
both backhoes lurch forward to cheers, our suppertimes.
Snow boots go on and on, off and on, then off. We hire
the neighbor kid, joke about Belize. We tease the guy across
the street about his half-assed pile, squint up at the roof's
death-swords of ice, come in for hot showers, hot chocolate,
bourbon, the milk and bread that panic bought. Back in the
before time, back when anything got to us. When we could
still feel. We move—so slow!—through Brady-sized drifts,
Gronks and Gronks of snow. We recite Dave Epstein, weatherman
poet, close read every tweet. Marvel at the physics of snow
banks, shovel-carved alleys, snow mazes, snow sofas, snow walls.

# Small Pleasures

"I don't think the wreath is big enough."
—Dr. LaShaun Williams, at the wreath-laying ceremony for the
enslaved peoples of Mount Vernon

There's a map of the bodies they've found so far, bodies
in coffins, we are told, coffins freed slaves were paid
to build. They want us to know the slaves were paid
to build them, that one of the slaves here was freed
in Washington's will, given thirty pounds a year,
buried here in an unmarked grave like all the rest.
They don't know the other ones' names, don't know
how many there are, but this is the guy they want us
thinking about. On the Enslaved People Tour our guide
calls whipping *discipline.* One woman says *So they
got food and clothing and a place to sleep.* As if
she's laying out fresh terms, some universal rights. *Also rape!*
I say, brightly, which makes me feel better, anyway.
Making white people feel better: what today is all about. One plaque
in the Women's Slave Quarters, labeled "Small Pleasures,"
includes *jew harp* and *clay pipe: people here enjoyed playing
music and smoking tobacco. In 1798, one Mount Vernon visitor watched about 30
slaves compete in Prisoner's Base, a team version of tag.*

# Basic Writing Skills

For their final papers, they had to write
a thesis and a counterargument. Anything.
Up to them. Forced narcotics counseling is wrong.
Getting raped by your stepfather can make you gay.
A letter to the parole board balancing
innocence and remorse. One prisoner
did all his assignments in Spanish, translated them
at night instead of sleeping. His argument
was to his son, in a Puerto Rican juvie on a drug charge.

*While I was not there for you when you were growing up,*
*you should not make the same mistakes I made.*

He worked on it for weeks, paragraphs with claim,
evidence, and analysis to say he was sorry, he thought
it was easy money, knows his son still thinks
it is, though no money could be harder: mothers
dead, fathers separated from sons, imprisoned
in different countries, unlikely to ever see each other again.
The last day they all read their papers out loud
while I stood with my back to the bumpy chalkboard.
When he finished I was too choked up to talk,
and they were watching when I wiped my eyes.

*Hey, professor, what, we gotta make you cry*
*to get an A in here? You want to cry?*
*I could tell stories that'd make you sob.*

# Sonnet for Academic Freedom

I walk through seven doors to teach in jail,
swipe my ID and go see who shows up.
They each get copies of *Bullets into Bells*
and notebooks, learn to annotate and stop
saying they aren't any good at writing, or they
don't read so well. I flirt with all of them,
plus guards, praise hair and lisps, poems and essays
on gun violence, parole, jail ed, and freedom.
I pass out pencils, take them back when time's
up, *so no one,* one C.O. says, *gets stabbed
in the eye.* They're all afraid of failure, so I
say they can revise all they want. So the bad
thoughts start to ease back up, let them work
in silence, breathing, focused—one break in the week.

# Barcodes

Nazis tattooed workers to keep them straight.
They died too fast for uniforms to work. We do it

with orange jumpsuits, prison scrubs. Goths
and Romans tattooed people they enslaved, and early on

we did that too: FUG for Fugitive, R for Runaway.
We tattooed criminals, or branded them. Today

we talk about tagging immigrants. Last year
we caught a man tattooing women with bar-

codes, what he said that they still owed. *Fuck
You, Pay Me* on her unlined neck,

a moneybag on one slim arm. *ATM* twists
across an inner thigh; a barcode mars a wrist.

# Campsite, Shenandoah

Days of kalmia, azalea, Blue Ridge. Nights
of steak on the grill, canvas chairs with cupholders,

cans of Stag and Blatz, Schlitz we lift from ice.
The fork in the firepit, stainless steel gone ember orange.

When I think it's cool enough, and clean,
I test it to my cheek.

Slender, distinct pain of tines, delicately seared:
a fight with a badger. Faux-tribal scarification.

The next morning the light gives me away, and Josey
laughs, starts calling me Tiny. As in *tines.*

A branding. Brand that reads as *shin* in Japanese:
kanji for *heart,* for *tenderness.* Tenderness

for my own rash heart. Heart of stupidity. Heart
of consequence. Crisp heart to spite my face all week.

# Testicles at Trinity, the Atomic Testing Site

Trinity, the atomic testing site, is open one day
a year. So we stay in a Socorro Super 8, eat green chile
cheeseburgers three meals out of four. We sing *don't want
no scrubs* to scrub oak and tumbleweed, get up early, get
in line. We drive through the White Sands Missile Range;
men with guns say don't take any pictures and I say
okay but I lie. *It's my country,* I tell Josey, shrugging,
breaking the law, imagining each person in each RV
around us saying pretty much the same thing. If you're
wondering who goes to Trinity, the atomic testing site, the one
day a year they are open, it's us. Also a lot of white guys
with Geiger counters we start calling *Geiger guys.* They are so
stoked to find trinitite, pick it up with their bare hands, put it
in the pockets of pleated khakis, right down next to their balls.
Trinitite is illegal. Trinitite was a mistake, a sort of bonus.
About to blow up the first atom bomb, some thought it might
ignite the atmosphere, burn the whole planet down. But
fuck it, right? Let's find out! Which, isn't that just so
us? But God—*knock, breathe, shine; break, blow, burn*—was
merciful, gave us a new element instead: Alamogordo glass,
atomsite, trinitite. White sand and *really* high heat. And with
this second chance what did we go and do? We made jewelry,
souvenirs. At the museum you can see necklaces on women—think

46

*oh god thyroid thyroid*—flash low on the front of her neck. *The blast*
*lifted sand into the air, melted it and then showered droplets* over miles.
We see one old man stretched out to get a photo of trinitite *in situ,*
his shirt tugged to bare soft white of belly here on the desert
floor. White sand and wonder. White sand and a really slow burn.

# The Creation Museum

Petersburg, Kentucky

God made the world. And He made it *awesome!*
Before the fall, before Adam and Eve fucked

everything up, *the animals didn't die. The people
didn't die.* In dioramas animatronic cave kids play

with animatronic dinosaurs. *Then the perfect world began
to suffer.* In film strips we see skulls, small pox, tanks,

a mushroom cloud. Way to go, Adam! Thanks a lot,
Eve! Here's what creationists love: fossils, dinosaurs,

Jews. What they still hate: Obama, people who ask
where Cain's wife came from, the separation of church

and state. The creationists just want to give you
hope: life isn't meaningless! Because you have hope

through Jesus Christ. This makes me sad
for them, embarrassed; who knew their lives

lack meaning? They need the Bible to be true, and
they need for us to care. I don't care. I love me

some Jesus, love a world that hires actors to play
the soldiers who killed him, love them

saying they were *just doing their jobs.* I love
watching these people cast around for ways this world

can prove the Bible's all true. So defensive about Cain
fucking his sister, so sure there were pet dinosaurs.

# Hell Fuckin' Yeah: SmackDown! vs. Raw

for Stacy Isenbarger and Alexandra Teague

*Smackdown AND Raw. Mexicans coming out*
*on John Deere tractors.* Strippers in boots
adorned with flames. Male strippers. *Chip*
*and Dales. An oil tycoon*—not an oil
tycoon—*steps from a limousine*
with his blonde be-moled young wife *to fight*
*Darth Maul.* Not Darth Maul. *His face was*
*made up like Darth Maul.* Okay. He
rips the mole off the tycoon's wife
and eats it. She's upset. Then *this*
*bucket of earthworms* is dumped on him
from the sky, or scaffolding. (Stacy
squints here, shows how he chews the ones
what land in his Darth Maul mouth.) At the
commercial break, the staff runs in,
folds up the paper the excess worms
fell on. *It is amazing. One*
*guy has this huge fist, and you see*
*it, smoke coming out. It happened.*
*It truly did. So you should go.*

# Dictionary Poem

I love teaching people how to use a dictionary,
watch them get faster than out-of-practice me,

watch them learn *ambivalent* or *incarceration,*
use them in their own new sentences. I teach men

and women in jail how to annotate a text,
underline the words that they don't know yet.

look them up in dictionaries I bring in for them to keep. *Indigo,*
*heft, cobbles, ostensibly:* words they learn while we go

through stories, essays, poems. Kings used to make
water magic by pouring it over carved tablets, then take

the water in their mouths to make carved words come true.
These students run their fingers over the lines, move

their lips to make the words belong to them:
*allure, billow, gypsum, joist. Resentment* and *regret.*

# Blank Verse for Bergdorf Goodman

"They had purses in the shape of elephants."
—Linda Mikula

They had purses in the shape of elephants.
They had denim slippers, a little distressed,
as if they were torn in the coral while they dredged
a treasure of crystals, pearls of every size.
Wide-heeled nude and black patent leather pumps,
flower-embellished, child's drawing of a shoe
from the 1940s. They had dresses made
from Union Jacks, full skirts with apron ties.
They had coin purses with googly eyes so the zip
became a mouth, pursed shut or brassy-grinned.
They had a café that looked out on the sun
in Central Park, toile wallpaper with green birds,
blue skies. Lobster napoleons. Fat slice
of truffle on each seared scallop. Rare duck breast
arranged on a gingery slaw. Mango panna
cotta, berries the size of your eyes. They had scarves
the size of blankets in ikat cashmere
so fine you could pull them through a ring, dresses
by people whose names I can't pronounce.
Walking around in there for long enough

you could learn a new language: Givenchy,
Louboutin, that guy who does the things
with diamond skulls. They had a diamond skull
chrome purse filled up with chain so heavy you
could lock your bike up with it or just up
and kill a man. They had brass knuckles pronged
with colored gemstones attached to a clutch,
so when you punch anyone who tries to take
it you are holding it really tight. They had
beaded skeletons dangling off dark coats,
wild pink fur-lined sandals—not shearling but loose
curls, almost tangled, as if the sheep had lost
twelve rounds, or rose from the dead, washed in the blood
of the lamb. Mannequins with kitten heads
both lifelike and human-head size. So, both cute
and tripping balls. They had jackets and skirts
printed with old engravings of faraway towns,
herds of someone's cattle, upside down
then right side-up, reflecting each other like
a shimmery pool. They had ladies in heels
and silk floral onesies, drinking champagne.
And the three of us, laughing, walking out, wack-
ass trousseau winging north, tax-free, concrete,
plus those bright hours, wonders we had seen.

# Horrors All Around

When I give the ladies on probation
apocalyptic fiction, ask them to write
their own, their future blown to hell, they get
ideas. Vampires, zombies, zombie ghosts,
the flu that wouldn't quit, how no one knows
the world's ending until it's almost gone.
The worst writer, the woman whose stare is most
opaque, the one who *I don't knows the most,* her
story's three words long: *Horrors all around.*
When asked what kinds of horrors, her eyes
go wide. She shakes her head. That's it.
There isn't any more to say. Just
*horrors.* Horrors all around. I say her story
needs more detail, that she should add specifics.
I pretty much just always want more nouns.
I point to her classmates' fevers, beat up RVs,
electric shocks in the flood. She doesn't budge.
But when I tell my friends about the class,
the scariest story's hers. Its silence, the barred
door of it, refusing to let the reader in to see. Horrors.
What horrors? Real horrors. All around.

# Whiteness in Bloom

Thinking about whiteness, what it is and what
it does, we go to the MFA to see Art
in Bloom. Groups of white suburban women,
garden clubs, look at art, arrange some flowers
to look like the art. Or something. Lilies scattered
over scaffolding: the Rape of the Sabine Women;
a column of callas: the Dead Body of Christ.
Older white women figuring out the flowers always
crack me up. One group looked at a boat of flowers
under a portrait of an Asian guy and was like *huh?*
So one of the ladies read the description, pointed to it,
said *You can read about him. He's a tradesman*
*from China. So kinda. . . that's a boat.* I text that
to myself, say it again, delighted. This is the kind
of whiteness I've come to see. We go every year, think
it's hilarious, like seeing parodies of our slightly
older selves, a little richer, continuing to come
here but without irony. There are phrases
from my southern youth about whiteness I remember:
*Mighty white of you; Free, white, and 21.*
Whiteness was aspirational. Sometimes I wanted more:
more whiteness like more money, the whitest kids
with ski passes from Vail on jacket zippers all winter long.

Invited to be a debutante, join a sorority, I said no,
explained I couldn't join an all-white group. *They have*
*their own groups,* other white people told me, exasperated,
leaving me in confused tears. It's embarrassing, talking
about whiteness. A hard job, imagining who you want
to be as an adult, barely knowing what it is
you don't want to have ever done.

# What Matters

My corner. My alma mater. Your
street. This endangered fish. Even when we
are patronizing we say *Sure, honey* like
*of course poetry matters.* Polo, quilting, Côtes
du Rhône. Civility Matters. But not
this! This bridge too far, where we go
*Well hold on just a minute.* One minute
matters, *cotton-picking* or no. Every second
counts. Count the pennies, the dollars will fuck
themselves. If someone says my *house matters my
yard my mother's health* we say *of course!* Not
*all houses, all streams, all childhood summer camps:*
too rude. *All schools matter,* we don't say. All
fish. Does Montana matter? Vermont? When I
first heard *Black Lives Matter* I thought it fell
too short. A rhetorical gesture, making a point, like
but surely we can all agree on this. A starting line.
Syntactically? It works like *Even Black Lives Matter,* not
*Black Lives Are More Important,* or *Black Lives: Holy
Holy Holy.* It doesn't even go as far as *Black
Is Beautiful,* way quieter than a fist of *Black
Power.* Just a little shrug. *Like hey guys at least we all agree
on this. Right, guys? Guys?* Even the least of these: cool,

cool. Even *His eye is on the sparrow:* no prob. Hey,
you! You with all the guns and all the power! You agree
that Black Lives at least *Matter,* right? Not really. Not
so much. But when I thought it was too gentle, I still
thought Hillary would win in a landslide, thought Nate
Silver was always right, still felt okay about identifying
as white. Whiteness a kind of mild joke, then: white bread,
mayo, American cheese. Black Lives Matter fell short,
I thought, when we kept seeing people shot. *Stop
Killing Us* I thought was more pointed, a better start.
But that was then, when I was so dumb. So innocent
and so guilty, and so wrong so wrong so wrong.

# A Cincinnati Stripper Bar

When we hear Cleveland's Caravaggio's
being cleaned we make plans for Cincinnati,
call a Cincinnati stripper bar a consolation
prize. I ask my students *So why's a Cincinnati
stripper bar better than a Dayton stripper bar?*
and they answer correctly: sibilance, assonance,
the extra foot. We buy notebooks and postcards
at the Cleveland Art Museum shop, eat at tableclothed
tables with ice water and heavy silver, drink wine.
Sour cream potato chips at an Ohio rest stop,
retirees on buses, Corvetted couples, the
*eloquent buffet* the hotel promises at breakfast
so we can get the hell on the road. We pass
Kent State, a place, a thing that happened two years
to the day before I was born. The Cleveland Art
Museum's treasures: *Stag at Sharkey's,* a Persian tent.
The lady concierge of our fancy hotel says the only one
around is in Kentucky, says it's *small, sad,
and stretch marky.* So, you know, no thanks. I like
my strippers unionized, glad to be there, earning
a share of the take. We remember how sad we were
to learn Platinum Plus in South Portland's not for happy,
ample-bodied blondes. So we skip the Cincinnati

stripper bar, go out for steak, for sundaes, strip down to swim in an over-chlorinated pool, sleep in a Cincinnati room.

# Notnames at the Detroit Institute of Arts

At the Detroit Institute of Arts the Caravaggio's no
great shakes. Mary Magdalene's face looks wrong—too

smooth, cartoonish compared to the draped silks and her
hand real, thoughtful on the mirror. But The Master

of the St. Lucy Legend, Master of the Embroidered Foliage—long
ago we lost their names, still praise what they were known

for with notnames. "Notnames": a real word I learned
for writing this. I think my favorite is Il Cronaca—The Chronicler.

That guy went to Rome the one time. Back in Florence,
he would not shut up about Roman ruins. Roman ruins

this, Roman ruins that: they forgot his real name.
Probably out of spite. There's more: Master of the Games,

of Saint Cecilia. And then the Rivera Courtyard. Rivera: Master of What?
Sturdy bodies, monuments, monumental workers. Real faces tucked

in every corner. Good enough we didn't throw it out
when he painted Lenin in that other one, gathering a crowd.

# Free Will, Faith, and Fungus

I like free will and faith, like figuring
it out. I like being able to tell who's a douche
by how they use the Lord. In Utah I read
about this con man with golden plates who made
fresh Bible with magic glasses—not even glasses!
Just rocks he named, saw through to read gold plates
nobody saw but him. Here's what I love
about Joseph Smith: he didn't even try.
The more ridiculous the story the more
likely that it's true. Why would he say those
ordinary rocks were magic? If
you want to make up magic rocks, at least
pick emeralds, diamonds, cool volcanic ones,
quartz you can see though. In the beginning of the Book
of Mormon, after he lists all the men who back
him up, so scared of getting smote, Smith says
to *ponder it in your hearts.* Hands it back over!
Ask him yourself! No pressure. The guy's a genius,
a piece of American work.

                          When my great aunt drives
from Sugarhouse to Liberty Park to show
me a tree where the Virgin of Guadelupe appeared,

I climb the rickety staircase, pass the candles,
check out the fresh cut where the shape, the saint
and mantle, had been: someone cut it off
to keep for himself. Or keep the crowds away.
When I get back to the car she shrugs and says
*It was just some kind of fungus.* I laugh, give my great-
aunt hell. *How else was God supposed to put
it there, Mary Jo?* And we imagine a sandaled
giant, stepping over Oquirrhs, Wasatch,
bending over to draw a Virgin with a magic
glowing pencil. Ridiculous. *Some kind
of fungus:* isn't that more amazing?  The ordinary,
raised up. Ordained, made fresh to order.
American fungus: something a great God would do.

# Donuts in Kidjail

Here is how often you see donuts in kidjail: never. Zero
times. Like seeing a cat or a dog, a cell phone. A white
kid, a comfy chair. Just me and this one kid, same kid
who wrote *Monkey Rescue* first time we worked together.
He saved Junior from a fire, then they got high by the pool.
I drew hearts and stars in the margins, helped spell "monkey,"
wrote *GREAT JOB!* They gave this kid two donuts, a small
carton of milk, and we wrote imitations of "One Art," me
with no breakfast yet. My stomach growled. The kid
looked up, both of us remembering I have a body. That
everybody gets hungry, whether or not they are free.
This cracked us up, and he offered me a donut. So I said
*You are a sweetheart and I am never going to eat your donut.*
Which made no sense to him. *Dude, I have a car and money—*
*I can walk out of here and buy a dozen as soon as you finish*
*this poem.* So he kept working. An empty classroom, "One Art,"
sharp pencil, still room. *What are some things you have lost?*
Mother, Father, Sister. Grandmother, school, ring. Country.
Bracelet. My stomach kept growling, we kept laughing, he
kept offering me a donut. Donut as distraction. Donut:
a gift. Finally he said *Look, I'm going to go pee. Then you*
*can eat the donut with no one watching.* Donut as test!
He left, and I said to the guard, *Hey I'm going to eat*

*that kid's donuts real quick-like while he's gone.* And the guard
was horrified, said he'd give me five bucks to not touch
the kid's donuts, explained donuts are hard to come by
in juvie, blah blah blah blah donuts. While I'm like *I WAS JUST
KIDDING! I WOULD NEVER MESS WITH THE PRECIOUS
DONUTS!* Kid came back, and we finished his draft, which
he asked me to keep till next time. And I drove away, past
Forest Hills and new condo construction, Blissful Monkey
yoga studio, Whole Foods. Parked my car and walked into my
house, where no one hurts me, where I eat whatever I want.

# My History of Lead

The Romans love it. Sweet and sour
in wine, sprinkled as salt on their suppers. Decline
and fall, poor Romans: go crazy. Let every wonder
burn. Turn to all of Europe, watch us learn
to poison our own. The French call it *poudre*
*de la succession,* a quick and easy way to get
to what we want. Come over here, to almost now:
we opaque our paint with it, make it quick to coat,
a glossy pleasure on the brush, until our babies take
up flakes from windowsills, doorjambs. We put it
in our gas, give it more oomph, less knock,
smooth the ride in cars as big as boats, smooth
as riding rails that we don't bother to build.
Bad faith; we undermine our us, write our progress
off. In Flint for years the cars pour off the lines
in flocks, in shining lots. Now the sudden river
slips into pipes and spreads from house to house
while people sleep. And here we are, a stack of easy
metaphors: declining, falling, the bodies of the poor
all pave the way, their leaders knowing better,
knowing best. What we know and when we know it.
What we do for money, for a little bit of cash.

# Monticello Visit Sonnet

"Black life is cheap, but in America black bodies are a natural resource
of incomparable value."
—Ta-Nehisi Coates, *Between the World and Me*

We love our country, all its fathers, times.
Jefferson and his best friend's shared grave
under a favorite oak: pretty gay. Which is fine
with us. We worried they'd gloss over the enslaved—
not mention the math he did on *their increase,* how
that all worked out. But then we see the place
is so small, everyone there must have known.
Getting Sally Hemings pregnant? More slaves.
Smart baby slaves, fresh-bred to look like you.
I ask a docent which people he picked to sell.
Did he keep his kids? *He might have wanted to
but there wasn't the money for it.* Right; *money.* Ah, well.
What he did for his country. What we do for ours.
What we think *family* means. And what money's for.

# Putting the *Oh, Christ* Back in Christmas

*I got you,* the waitresses and bartenders of the South
say this year, on our old-people holiday road trip.
American treasures, lynching memorials at the Equal
Justice Initiative's Legacy Museum, Montgomery,
Andersonville, plantations, some founding fathers'
homes. We say we are putting the Christ back
in Christmas, if by Christ you mean executed innocents.
*O My America:* nothing says *Holiday!* like fighting
with men about whether Sally Hemings was raped,
what "concubine" means, fourteen. One wants to tell us
how wrong we are about most everything we know.
When he says, knowingly, a grown-up to two women
of the world, *I mean, we don't <u>know</u> it was rape,* Josey
and I don't look up from our plates, don't need to decide
to fuck with this guy. We both just get to it, like breathing.
*I got you,* waitresses, bartenders say, and we soothe
the twitch in his Faulkner-looking mustache: *of course
Jefferson didn't think he was a rapist.* This makes him relax
so much he agrees when Josey shrugs, says *I mean, she
was bred for it, right?* Then he sees what we have done.
Too late! In Andersonville the graves stretch out
for acres, each with a red-ribboned Christmas wreath,

reach as far as the eye can bear. In Americus Jimmy Carter teaches Sunday School; a king-size bed in a Red Roof Inn sets you back sixty bucks. In the morning you can see everything. In the morning you can see what we've done.

# I Imagine the Butches' Stripper Bar

At my butches' stripper bar you can watch butches
fold laundry, iron. Objectify them while they
slowly refinish a roll-top desk, take off a trailer hitch.
They file taxes, wear waders, bake you a layer cake.
*I'll lay her cake,* my imagined patrons mutter. I think
of who I eroticize, how: they're always getting stuff done.
At real stripper bars the women just dance; so many things
they could be checking off their lists. I guess men don't want
to see women work?  They get that at home?  In my Champagne
Room the butches plant bulbs, build bookshelves, clean
basements, write checks to the ACLU, re-train
your dog. Fantastic grow the flannel plaids; they lean
and squint, lick pencils, adjust a miter box. They
make box lunches, chicken stock. The butches make your day.

# What Kids Don't Know

I visit a high school and the high school kids
ask if I still write poems for Josey. I didn't

remember kids don't know the grown-ups all
around them are in love. Their schlubby principal

in his cluttered office. Tired cafeteria ladies
in hairnets, smelling like Tater Tots. All these

coaches and waiters, all the doctors and great-aunts.
People working drive-thru windows! They smile, they hand

you paper cups filled up with popcorn ice. They were up
all night in bed with someone they can't get enough of,

can't stop thinking about. They are making some mental lists.
Enough going on upstairs to last all through a double shift.

Your librarian is writing a love letter. She is smiling, saving it
on her laptop, sighing. And now she is touching her lips.

# Reason to Live

Gas $1.99 in Ohio. Soft
green fields, green forest.
Retirees smile at rest stops,
and we laugh, *that's us*

*in ten years.* If we're
lucky. The heartbroken
kids behind the bar
with Josey say we give them

a reason to live: so
in love we are
happy to drive through Ohio.
Happy to be where we are.

Three

# Spelling "Prostitutes"

I volunteer at a juvie, call it kid-
jail. We play a homemade Boggle, make all the words
we can, make Mad Libs things with them like this:
*lip split from slipping in shit, I sit and sip*
*spilt spit.* We write Fast Poems, Rescues, give
a lot of high fives. One kid loves Fun Facts,
one What Would You Do With Five Million Dollars,
but then just says he'd give it to foster kids.
Fun-Facts wants to buy the building, a bulldozer, knock
the whole fucking kidjail down. Good call. I
make him write a shopping list: *crowbar, hard*
*hat, boots,* say he could rent a wrecking ball.
A third says he'd spend his on, *how do you say*
*it, pro-to-tute?* He doesn't speak English so hot,
doesn't know "grown-up," "omit": *PROSTITUTES,*
I say, *P-R-O-S*—spelling it for
him, cracking up, until Fun-Facts says *Miss, that's*
*because he WAS a prostitute.* Some split
seconds in kidjail I trip over, slip
in my pocket to ponder later, indulge my rage
or tenderness. I want to bulldoze down
the house where he was hurt, re-set to spin
him back into an unharmed toddler, pluck

his plump self up and hide from what, from here,
we know will happen. I want to beat a pimp
to death with a crowbar, rent a wrecking ball.
But we only have an hour or so, an hour
that's not about me or my precious, privileged, white-hot
lily-white heart. So I spell "prostitute" for a kid
who was a prostitute—or maybe not,
maybe none of these boys has ever been hurt,
maybe Fun-Facts is fucking with me. I spell
"prostitute" and say *Oh, man,*
*you guys are so much more generous than me:*
*I was going to buy a villa in Venice.*
Then they ask *What's a villa?* and *Where is Venice?*
And I draw Italy on typing paper,
describe the Grand Canal and watery alleys,
and floating up to columned villas on long
wooden boats, write *GONDOLA, CANAL,*
and *VENICE,* say they can visit my *VILLA,* bring
all their foster kids, their prostitutes.

# American Treasure

My students in jail are experts in getting in their own
way, destroying what they're mad at most:

themselves. But also racism! Some things it makes more sense
to hate. They're invisible, trapped by shorter sentences.

They write about jail, prison, America, gun violence.
We laugh about everything: white privilege,

when we're going to die, drugs—"Jill, do you do coffee before
you come in here?" "Nope! Just a *leetle* bump of coke." I swear,

sit with the distracted ones, say *shut your mouth and do
your work*, point to the text we're at, write *I AM SO*

*PROUD OF YOU* when they get something right. I draw hearts
and stars. *High five!* I love them. Men and women trying to start

fresh. People we keep trying to throw away. I love their easy laughs
in impossible circumstances: nothing more American than that.

*I was in prison and you visited me,* says Christ. *Give*
*without worry,* the new Pope says. They let me see my privilege

everywhere: my car, my house, my bed. This face cops love.
These unbruised arms. Getting to call everybody *sweetheart* or *hon.*

# Whitman at the Huntington

Josey and me in a plane, a taxi; Josey and me in a Lyft. Hours
in L.A., its jacaranda, oleander, Steely Dan on a loop in our

heads. Orange groves and roses in the cool of the morning: West
Coast mornings, even I'm awake. Bust of Dante, bust

of Sir Bacon, Emmy and Morex and Samuel at work
in the library, Samuel in a rose-patterned shirt.

Samuel says he only got to see Whitman's diary because
I requested it. We're still figuring out how to use our powers, what

our powers are. Josey and I march again, this time against ICE,
private for-profit prisons, kids parceled out all over the place.

Whitman's Civil War hospital diary is smaller than the palm
of my hand, filled with hurt boys all missing their moms

in makeshift hospitals. Stinking and sobbing, torn
up by human needs. Whitman furious at *the swarms*

*of contractors and their endless contracts and the paper*
*money*. American relic, context, American treasure.

Also his shopping lists: *forceps, scissors, sponge* at one moment. *Bottle of brandy, paper, horehound candy* in the next.

# Path to Nowhere

My neighbor stands on her back stoop, watches me stamp
on shovels, me sweat, me tug up trash trees in my yard.

This yard was all packed dirt, a crap-ass lack of grading.
One old syringe, a hundred broken bottles. She watches me

work. She loves to watch me work on my knees, digging, lifting,
flipping Goshen stone from pallets into pathways, raised

bed for the cherry, its silken iridescent bark. She sighs, *Whew!
A lot of work!* I smile the way that means *shut the fuck up*, get back

to, yes, a lot of work. When I finish settling flagstones, pat
their sun-warmed little backs, their gorgeous curves

a mica-gleaming weight from gate to barbecue, she brays
*A path to nowhere!*, a line I keep, use again and again. All

that work: a path to nowhere. A lush backyard: what's
the point? Poetry: a path to nowhere, outsiders not knowing

where we are. Here we are! I found us! On our paths, each
ambling along. Sometimes I cried, taught seven classes, cleaned

houses, painted them, waited tables, tended bar. Not true, not
really: I tended bar so badly, and for just a second—ask Misty,

anyone. I made gorgeous garnishes, achingly slow cocktails.
A path to nowhere, those cocktails. Like poetry, they got so

much nothing done. A path, though, a way, a way forward:
a way to think through our lives. Our lives, what we want

to do with them. Even my bitch-ass neighbor a gift,
a punch line, each piece a glinting, sun-warmed stone.

# Why They Hate Us

The rearview camera
is why they hate us. Active
Park Assist, so you can have
a car, not learn to parallel
park. Also Las Vegas, the decadent
West. All You Can Eat is why
they hate us, our fat ass falling
off the edges of our chair.
Our sturdy-ass chairs is why
they hate us, chairs that we sit in
to eat all we can. Gay marriage
isn't why they hate us, that shit
just makes no sense to them. Drones
is why they hate us. Unceasing sound
in the air, the women and children
and horses we kill. Calling them
"them" is why they hate us. Us
versus Them, over and over again.

# It Is What It Is Poem

If it is what it is then I hate it. If it is
what it is no it's not. What can you do? Just try
something. What can you do? Actually, a lot.

If it is what it is then shut up it. *It is*
*what it is* is a shrug. If it is what it is
then it isn't. *It is what it is?* What the fuck.

# Americus, Georgia

Josey looks up from the atlas and her phone,
says *Americus boasts three Mexican places!*
On our southern road trip for Civil War sites,
Civil Rights, in her Andersonville cap, Josey looks
like a retired dentist: you can almost see
the model trains in his basement. I always look
like a social worker. We learn something new
every day: how long it took to decide to enlist
Black soldiers. And then, to sum up, we won! Plaques
on dysentery, Nat Turner, those soldiers
traveling through the South telling enslaved
people *You're free.* In the motel's *USA
Today*s there's more about the wall to keep
Mexicans out of America; the Mexican restaurants
of Americus are friendly, delicious, jammed:
clearly we need some more. We turn Black soldiers down
for months when they could have helped us win
so much faster. And one out of three Black baby
boys we slam into jail, when we need them so much.
Those kids at the border, sick babies in Flint:
all those future engineers and jokers, big
yawners, social workers and dentists, dog

lovers, bespoke tailors and whistlers. Historians, back-sassers, street-smilers, sad readers, teenagers. Good reporters. More of everything we need.

# Candlelight Christmas at the Plantation

On the Christmas Candles Tour of Monticello
everyone's ready for glamour, romance. A party!
So we get eggnog, chamber music, port.

Here's Jefferson on slave revolts: *I tremble*
*for my country, when I reflect that God is just.*

Also, his best business tip? Buy more Black
women. One *who brings a child every two years*
*is more profitable than the best man of the farm.*

At Monticello, in the flicker and chill,
we coo over moldings, chairs *of his own design,*
walk around the snow-covered unmarked graves,
uncounted people he enslaved.

                    In the summer
*escape* there's still a staircase from his chamber pot
down to the slave basement. But here it's gone, those dark
rooms a floor below opening to night
air instead of up to his bed. Our tour

is filled with what's unsaid: whist by the fire
and *profitable* rape, *mighty near white* Sally's
young sons making nails, hauling wood, while white
grandkids play the Royall Most Pleasant Game
of Goose. Its spiral path and obstacles:
the Grim Reaper, the Dungeon, and the Maze.

# Lucky Copper Smelter

I see the Red Line rise and cross the salt
and pepper bridge, think *lucky.*
Copper smelter on the horizon,
edge of Oquirrhs, that's lucky too.
Lucky bracelet, lucky bridge. Once
on a Mexican highway I pulled
over to the shoulder, needed to get
my lucky bracelet at once from the trunk.
Plastic millefiori beads of dinged
and dingy plastic, medallion of the *Virgen,*
pinkie nail-sized Christ on the Cross.
When I caught vintage glass beads in midair
at Mardi Gras, their cool pressure quick
in my hand, I knew that they were lucky.
Women turned to stare and want. Lucky
they didn't take out somebody's eye.
The sound of the beads on my wrist
forever after: echoes of mahjong tiles,
dominos, rosaries, poker chips, ice.

# What a Waste

I tell Josey *I'm going to write and publish*
*a poem about your breasts called "What*
*a Waste"* and she says *Don't forget my ankles.*
It's true; her ankles are sculpted, sharp
and sleek and hollowed just where they should
be, cry out for high heels. *They're something*
*out of film noir,* I tell her. *No,* she says, *they're*
*a fucking Bernini.* What every woman wants:
ankles and breasts like Josey's, Josey's perfect
body wasted in Carhartts, Jockeys, Pendleton
shirts. I want to gnaw on her left ankle like a
chicken leg, anybody would, and don't get me
started on her breasts. But Josey's delicious,
compact body isn't for us, gang: Josey gets
to do whatever she wants with hers.
*What a waste,* I tell her, while we laugh
at whoever would say such a thing about
someone else, another *person,* or her perfect
body, Josey using it to live her perfect life.

# Reading "What a Waste" to College Boys

I write a poem called "What a Waste" about Josey,
about how even though sometimes I want to devour
her whole, it's up to her what happens to the only
body she has. I think this is a funny poem. I think
I'm making a joke about consent, desire, marriage.
Maybe lesbian bed death? Middle age? I don't know.
This may be too meta, even for me. Anyway, I read it
to some students while I'm a visiting writer. Two white
boys raise their soft and earnest hands—*so young!*
—want to share with me and everyone else
in the room their wide-eyed stories, how sometimes girls
with beautiful bodies just don't want to fuck them.
They both spoke with a kind of wonder, like I get it,
right? Like, how can that even *be?* And we shook
our heads at the sad injustice of it. Sometimes even I
can't tell when I am kidding anymore. I said *I know,
man. Other people's bodies aren't for us. It sucks, right?*
And they nodded, taking that in, thinking it over, I guess
for the very first time. Poetry, getting so much nothing done.

# Would Pile

My dad posts a video of a fallen tree and two dogs,
Bucky and Roscoe. *Roscoe,* he says, *what do you think*

*about that big log?* He pans the length of the thing,
forty feet of hardwood still in tree form. Roscoe

grins. Bucky has jumped up top. The woods
in Alexander, North Carolina are beautiful, light

doing all the woods-things light does: dappling,
falling in shafts, glittering on leaves that sparkle

green and greener. What is my father thinking?
Wood flooring? His bronze sculptures of ladies

in wood? A chain saw, a splitter, all the firewood
in the world? Wealth, possibility, future in lichen-

covered bark a red oak about *3-4 foot at the butt*
*with a nice straight trunk 35 foot before a big branch.*

# Rosa Parks Edits Her Statement as She Writes It

"I had been pushed around ~~for~~ all my life ~~becau~~ and felt at this moment that I couldn't take it anymore. When I asked the policeman why we ~~were~~ had to be pushed around? He said he didn't know. "The law is the law. You are under arrest." ~~I acte I went will~~ I didn't resist."
—handwritten note from the Rosa Parks Archive, Library of Congress

*I had been pushed around for*
*what? Because why?* It doesn't
matter. The pushing? It's not
about her. *When I asked*
*the policeman why we were,*
we weren't. We weren't acting;
we had to *be pushed around.* Whether
I acted or not, *went willingly*
or not, it doesn't matter.
The point is, to resist all this?
Start out with *I didn't resist.*

# On the Deerfield River

*How long do I have to wait before I start living*
*the life I want?* Pauline says she asked herself
in Midtown, chucked it all and moved to Vermont.

Or one of those. New Jersey? I get them all confused. Chuck
takes me to the Hoosac Tunnel, once our longest, running under
the Berkshires. Chuck says hundreds died in its construction.

In my lack of imagination I see coal miners, the tunnel interior
fighting back, but when I look it up it's all explosions, black
powder to nitro, pod of pudding stone demoralized rock

the men all hated to dig: a *shovelful of eels.*
Walking toward the tunnel an early autumn afternoon
while the others get into their waders, rig up their gear, tie

on their flies, we look at each other wide-eyed when we feel
a basement chill, so sudden you can walk in and out of it,
shadow spilling into light. The train goes by on a tall

bridge over kayakers, men in poke boats, all of them doing
exactly what they want. We joke about Rachel's
fishing show, what her fishing show would be. Specials

on falling, spelling "Hoosac," 25 silent minutes to tie
a single knot. I love fishing, don't care what I catch.
I don't need the gear and hassle, love wearing waders in the river,

cool pressure of the current on my legs. I love finding
a muddy bank to lean on, a tufted hillock, a kind of tuffet just
for me. Or a big rock parting the water, probably blasted

from the tunnel, where I can perch and watch my best friends fish
and stumble, lurch into each other, laugh in the deepening light
on my face, my empty hands, sun angling out of William Blake.

# Rain and Gravy

I'm ready to leave the house when the rain
thickens, shifts from thin ribbons to fresh ropes
and I tell Josey I'm not taking the T, I'm calling
a Lyft, spending $20 on twenty minutes leaning back
with her arm around me, my cheek on her shoulder,
looking at silver chains of rain out the window.
Ribbons and streams, the shirr of it on the slope
of pavement, the distant knocking hulls of thunder
somehow under our house. Josey reads the *Globe,*
tells me about Gordon, how he loves alcohol
and marijuana, God love him, has the jacked athleticism
the Patriots desperately need. The *Browns are sick
of him,* she tells me. I am drinking tea, nestling back
into her, tangled in our torn Bates coverlet, linen
sheets. *It could be a no-risk acquisition,* she says.
*You're* a no-risk acquisition, I tell her, lazy joke
we've made a hundred thousand times. *You're* a wide
receiver, *you're* a tight end, weak defense, deflated
ball. You're the biggest hole in national football! You're
penetrating the end zone, pushing through that hole.
But she says *No—I'm not a no-risk acquisition.
I'm high risk. I'm old.* And I say *Yeah but I already got 20
years. You were a bargain. The rest of this is gravy.*

# Poetry Class in a Massachusetts Prison

Turner's lips twitch, his eyebrows go
crazy while he reads Jack Gilbert. I tell
Matthew to think *olive,* not *motor,* on the *ooze*
*of oil crushed.* Paulie's a skinny white guy, blond
beard, blue crocheted kufi cap, going to town
on Robert Hass's "Meditation at Lagunitas."
Which is hard to do! I ask Carl who's the "you"
in "One Art." Ben's shaking his head, erasing
all thought on John Clare. Butch just says *outstanding*
when I ask how he likes Gail Mazur's "Baseball."
He beams. They are men alone with poems, last day
of class in jail. Ken saying *Jill I can't do this, I'm no good*
*with poems.* And me saying *Ken shut up you give me that*
*crap every time I give you anything to do.* Ken laughs,
admits he gets the poem's loneliness, knows
what lonely's like. *I broke up with my ex-girlfriend*
*when I caught this sentence.* I roll my eyes and he gets it,
gets that he gets the poem. Last class. Goodbye,
my gentleman felons. Goodbye to their sentences, locked
cabinets of books we're not allowed to use. Goodbye
dark clothes two sizes too big. Men trying their best, their

beat-up desks. Their glasses and watches, all of us
working together, in the time we have left. Shrugging
at pages, holding their heads in tattooed, winter-dry hands.

# Aphasia Sonnet for the Black Seed Writers

*I can feel it before the world comes out*
Katharine says, and we both laugh, because
she means *the word*, of course, but *the world's* about
as close as we can get. The writers buzz
in St. Paul's basement: homeless poets quick
to pick up trochees—*DO-nuts, COF-fee*—psyched
to try new skills, write Larkin-y quatrains sick
of the Orange Line, its office types, their handi-wipes.
I love handi-wipes, drink coffee, help
them scan and get that *Katharine* looks like three
but she says *KATH-rine*, so it's a trochee as well.
Katharine wants me to know about her head injury;
I say all these words—*stress, line breaks*—are hard won
and the last couplet's like *Law and Order's DUN-DUN.*

# Remembering the Old World

I've already forgotten smoking on planes, how we found
out anything before Google. *555 1212,* a kind
of all-knowing operator who could tell you your friend's
mom's number in Nashville, all the drugstores in Des Moines.
And now how long since I leaned into a stranger on the bus?
How long till I touch a shoulder in a bar? My mother once asked
a stranger about her ice cream cone. She offered my mother
a lick. Hanging off a subway strap, laughing with strangers
in an airport bar. What tendernesses we can't have. What
we lost without knowing we loved it: the smell of your
friend's house at suppertime, warm dry hands exchanging
the peace at church. Handing people dollar bills and saying
*good luck* and they say *god bless you honey* back.
The metal detector in jail, clean sound of a stack of stapled
handouts aligned against a table with two taps. Killing time
in a T.J. Maxx. Cocktails someone else made. Shaking snow
off my hair in a vestibule, warm air on my red ears.
Smiling at a hostess. Josey waiting at the bar.

# Quarantine 2020

Packs of police shoot people with paint cans, rubber bullets.
They shoot at peaceful protestors, reporters, people filming
from their porch. We are all reporters, now that they have fired
the reporters. For ten weeks we've been up all night refreshing feeds

to understand a virus, to look at memes of how the virus now
is us, how nature makes a way. We smile at our neighbors
behind masks, wave to help each other know that we
aren't calling the cops. We praise a couple getting high in their car,

say *that's the way to do it* and the guy grins, squeaks out *antibodies!*
We donate online. NAACP, bail funds here at home and in Detroit,
Atlanta, Chicago, Louisville. Who knows when we can travel there

again? But while I click I get to remember Rivera murals
in Detroit, Seelbachs in Louisville. The lesser kudu at The Field Museum
with its taxidermied eyelash askew, like it just stumbled home
from some crazy kudu night out. Lesser kudu karaoke, lesser kudu prom.

When the motorcycle boys pop wheelies by the zoo
gates here, lions roar back from inside. No one's
allowed in to see them anymore. A zoo in Germany feeds
some animals to others, now it's Covid times. We wake

to sunlight on the same trees green in May breezes, skies
bluer for the lack of smog the no-more-traffic breeds.
Here there's birdsong, there a man's knee on a neck. Streets
are empty and then they're full, our streams full of full streets.

# One Day Over and Over

We see a dumb movie about one day over and over, ask
what day we'd pick. *Our wedding day,* Josey says, reflexively,
an easy win we laugh at—classic Josey—and also those days
kind of sucked. A civil union in Vermont before it was legal,
the backyard party we threw, stressed out the whole time. Then
the state-sanctioned one: first justice of the peace we called
said he wasn't sure yet about the gays. Nevermind, man! Don't
do us any favors, bub! But then we go through good days, one
walking from temple to shrine to matcha ice cream in Kyoto.
A birthday in Florence, when we probably had Covid but
didn't know it, walked from the Hotel Hermitage up
to San Miniato, down to the market at Santo Spirito, sucking
on Golia to stop coughing, buying all the vintage smoky plastic-
frame reading glasses we saw. Waking to cedars on terra cotta
embassy walls in Rome, hopping the tram from Maxxi
to Via Flaminia, walking to the Vatican past angels on bridges,
after the Berninis at the Borghese, long lunch at La Rosetta, quick
shade of the Pantheon. Was that all in one day? Could be.
Does it matter? What are the One-Day rules? Maybe it's Maine,
me thigh-deep in low tide holding onto the boat while Josey runs
over to Holbrook's for steamers and wine, a steak we grilled
on the rocks there once. A day we slept on our new porch sofa
outside, the day they said I could teach in the jail, or when

she defended her thesis, one of many days we found out whatever
that thing was wasn't cancer, or wasn't anymore. For now. So
we give up trying to pin down a Best Day; we can't. In the current
solitude, homemade masks and cherry jam, one day follows
another of iced coffee and reading, email and *what do you want
to get done today,* sourdough toast and *tell me how I can help.*

# My History of Vaccination

When Cotton Mather enslaved Onesimus,
he asked if he'd had smallpox. First he named
the man Onesimus, which means *useful*. Then he asked.
Employee intake: slavery HR. Onesimus, *a pretty
intelligent fellow,* and a *mighty smile of heaven upon my family,*
said *yes and no: an operation which had given him something
of the smallpox would forever preserve him from it.*
Onesimus! So helpful. Adding that *it was often used among
the Garamantese, and whoever had the courage
to use it was forever free from the fear of the contagion.*
In 1716 Mather wrote his friend about this, another guy,
who enslaved somebody else. Just two dudes writing
each other chipper letters about the people that they own.
Onesimus told Mather all about it, *showed me the scar,
and his description of it made it the same that afterwards
I found related unto you by your Timonius.*

Onesimus, Timonius. The fucked-up names enslavers gave
the men that they enslaved. So, inoculation: Mather stole
the idea from the guy he stole. And even then other Americans
hated him for that. Not the stealing, or enslaving, but the idea:
variolation was "negroish." People made fun of Cotton Mather
by naming their slaves "Cotton Mather." One guy threw a bomb

at Mather's house with a note that said *Cotton Mather, you dog,*
*dam you! I'l inoculate you with this; with a pox to you.*
We're so dumb. Dumb and evil, both, America. But *I'l inoculate you*
*with this* is pretty good. Eventually Mather let Onesimus go, sort of;
he had to come back *every Evening* to chop and bring in wood,
fetch water. Also, *in great snows, appear seasonably with the help*
*of the Shovel,* that sort of thing. Other than that, totally free. As
long as he gave Mather some money to buy someone else. Then
Cotton Mather bought a boy he named Obadiah. I can't figure out
how old he was, or where he came from, just that he was young.
And Mather named him Obadiah, which means a *Servant of the Lord.*

# Small and Large

Walking in the park with the pink seersucker veil
I made myself, past small glacial erratics and pudding stone
walls, I talk to Maggie on my AirPods. She tells me
about her air fryer, how it's bigger than mine. Bigger
than a bread box? Who knows? Maggie says *it's the size
of a small spaceship,* a really unhelpful comparison.
I point out that doesn't mean anything, average spaceship size
being only in her head. Like, *mine's the size of a coffee maker,*
I tell her. Helpful! Pointing out most people agree how big
a coffee maker is. What makes sense is that nothing makes sense
anymore. All we can do for each other is share recipes, crack
each other up. So much to remember and nothing to do. Wash
hands. Wipe down the keys and phone. At the beach ten feet apart
we tell Jenna and Carrie we can't focus, can't get even one whole
thing done. We go from a quarter clean kitchen to laundry half-
folded, finish an email we started yesterday, or Tuesday, start
in on the kitchen again. Before, I did whatever I wanted; finish
at the gym and decide if I'd read at a restaurant, have a long lunch.
I might go to the library or Athenaeum, work there, then go to a movie
or meet up for martinis, soup dumplings, pho. I used to float
through the city on whims and not notice. So now I give myself

whatever small choice I can. Do I want to finish the kitchen or start
in on the laundry? Deal with emails or make lesson plans? The way
we ask a toddler not *what do you want for dinner,* but *red plate or
the blue one?* Illusion of choice, a play world now the real one's gone.

# December Meeting Sonnet from in the Before, Room 47

We have whole meetings on what we cannot know:
two dozen writers in a room wondering
if anyone above us has a vote
about the future, money, forms for stumbling
through the present. Half of us have coughs.
Everyone has other work to do.
One of us remembers, sort of, stuff
about the past. One is still confused.
*If this, then that,* someone guesses. He
says it like he knows. Some people bark
with laughter, or more coughs. Maybe we
just want shared dazes, company in the dark.
*I'm with you!* one says. *Point blank! Full stop!*
He thanks the committee. Everyone looks at the clock.

# All the Deer in New Hampshire

All the deer in New Hampshire, two hyenas at the Denver Zoo:
Josey downloads the *Globe,* gives me the news

while I wake up. Russia's bad, and Minnesota. Colombia and Idaho.
Also Josey's coffee's too hot. *The hotness window is always a narrow*

*one,* she says. *Not for me, though, right?* I ask. *You're fifty years
hot,* she tells me, and I'm delighted: *My whole life so far?*

Hot in Judy's womb. Hot toddler, hot in sixth grade. But no:
Josey thinks I've got fifty years hot total. Starting when we met. So

when I'm seventy-five-and a half? Still hot. Seventy-six? *Then you'll just
be old.* I laugh, call *Asshole* after her while she goes to make another cup.

Outside is terrible: the deer, jails, numbers going up. Inside's bad too:
our dear teeth crumbling in our mouths, cancer probably twitching in a few

cells we care about, ours or someone else's. Middle age is sweet, for
now. *I'm having a good time,* I'd say out loud in the before, more

and more again these days. We were pretty good at recognizing joy when
we were younger, poorer, really very tired. But now we have more time. Broken

world full of horrors and a sun-soaked walk along the harbor. Drop
by Drop Greek wine and dollar oysters for lunch. For now. Until we stop

again with going out. Sparrows bounce on the cobbles of Black Lamb's patio.
The sweetheart who pours our wine has a new kitten; he named her Miso,

and shows us pictures on his phone. Miso's soft marmalade of fur, same shade
as his ginger beard. I taste the wine, nod, say *it tastes like wine!* Bouquet

of wine, frisson of fill 'er up. World enough, and wine, and all
the deer in New Hampshire. All the deer, hyenas, cats and dogs.

And ferrets. Fruit bats, minks, pigs, and rabbits have it now. Bank voles
and common marmosets. The house sparrows are still fine, still

bouncing on the cobbles. The wine's website says it's Roditis:
*Yummy. Clean citrusy, sharp, with roundness and fruit persistence.*

# Jealous of Children

Not jealous of people *with* children, children being both
expensive and delicate, a vanity project, like collecting vintage
Porsches, breeding racehorses. But, worse, actually jealous
of the children themselves. My friend Marie's feeling low, so
I tell her: in the middle of distancing I've become unhinged
with rage, pained by friends who I think don't love me
as much as I love them, think they love even the CHILDREN
of their better friends more than they love me. Me: some second
preference, twice removed. So now I am jealous of little kids
just trying to muddle through a plague: pathetic! The kids
go fishing with my old friends. Marie asks if I'm making that up.
But I see it on Instagram, the tiny images making me wince, me
over here healthy in my happy marriage with my stable income,
so much love and books and homemade pizza, cookie dough.
Zooming in on kids with their smooth perfect skin and fish, touching
my friends who don't text me back, kids who get to breathe in
their precious friend breath, leaning back, taking my friends' bodies
for granted. Bodies forbidden to me now, bodies I didn't know
how fiercely I loved. They are children in boats in cool water
in green shade that smells like rivers and I can't even write about it,
because then my friends will know that I am crazy instead of cool
with it, whatever, just their chill friend who will be here, a fully grown
calm adult, when this is all over. Just over here driving stick, stirring

martinis, using the word "amortize" in a sentence. Gonorrhea! *Goodfellas!*
*The Wire! Amuse-bouche!* I can talk about shotgun kissing old boyfriends
in truck cabs, VW Cabriolets. Can some eight year old do that? I tell Marie
all of this, Marie a safe place in the pandemic to stash my smallest
shames. Or rather, my biggest shame: of being small. And Marie, God
bless her holy name, says *Damn right you can. How many exes
can an eight year old even have, four or five? Amateur hour.*

# Ponkapoag Pond

Now we walk around outside instead of watching Netflix
on a treadmill at the gym. In the new uncertainty we know
so much more about our parks, our least-busy streets, best
ways to make a mask out of a T-shirt, an old sundress. We try
to go further, take a drive as a little treat, a trip to the suburbs'
leafy lanes and fat-roll ranches. The Ponkapoag Pond
parking lots are full, so we park on a side street, put on
our home-sewn masks to walk around the water
social-distancing style. We can see the water; we're
so close. But a woman runs out of her mid-century muffin top
to yell that we can't park in the wide expanse of fresh-asphalt
empty public road in front of her stupid house, calms down
only when she sees we are middle-aged white women like her,
waving and calling out *Thank you!* and *Sorry!* Back in the car
I'm frustrated enough to cry, to mutter *Fucken Ponkapoag
Pond bitch* under my mask, so she doesn't know. I start
laughing—first at myself and then darkly at race, American
myths of freedom, scarcity. So we fuck off back to the city
where we belong, walk the neighborhood, cross the Orange Line
tracks to Franklin Park, wave to city ladies on shady stoops
who say *I like your mask* and *Have a good day,* happy to talk

to us, to anyone. One shrieks *HI!* and then makes fun of herself, saying, *I'm like, HI, ANYBODY!* Cheerful! Making the best of things. Bighearted. Unlike me. Unlike that pinched-face bitch in her ugly house at Ponkapoag Pond.

# Freedom is My Pedicure

My haircut, my mask-free trip
to buy a brand-new toaster,
shoot that Black guy jogging
through my neighborhood. Oh my
America, you never fail to disappoint,
reveal yourself, our whole ass,
embarrass everyone. Every Katrina
and Covid a fresh chance for us
to show ourselves exactly who we are.

# There Was a Lot of Stuff to Do

And so I did it. Stuff needs doing! You just
have to do your stuff. I had to sit down some
cool place quiet and do it: emails, cut
a few lines off the revised syllabus and run
it past the committee co-chairs before we meet.
I had to reply to all the bullet points
by COB Friday, but first I needed
to see what's COB, and keep rags moist
with the CDC-provided recipe
for bleach solution. Wipe down my phone, doorknobs,
mail, shoes. Fill out the OneForm, submit receipts
with the W9 and the invoice, the Terra Dotta
pdf. Record me saying *Oh, hello;*
*I didn't see you there,* upload the video.

# We Pay Afghanis for the Afghanis
# We Kill

"Hearts, Minds and Dollars: Condolence Payments in the Drone Strike
Age" —*ProPublica,* 2013

What do they buy? A bicycle to replace what
we ran down. A car plus cash for the woman shot

at an unmarked checkpoint, woman in her own car.
Condolence payments, battle damage repair,

reparations, *solatia.* A cow, a sheep, another
sheep. A loom? Do they use looms? Whatever

they use. A funeral, a funeral debt. Tuition?
Three thousand for your left arm, right hand,

left eye. Three hundred ninety-two for your three-year-old
daughter's arm. Six thousand for your twelve year old.

*Consistent with the local custom:* nine hundred
for your wife, seven thousand for your son. *The*

*people we meet don't talk about the money so much—*
imagine someone coming to apologize, to touch

your shoulder, after all this. To write you a check. And
*how they felt when they shook someone's hand.*

# Just Once and All Wrong

On the Hemings Family Tour at Monticello, one man wants
to say out loud that, actually, slavery's mostly
been normal. *What about five hundred years ago in Germany!?*

*What about Rome!?* he barks. *WHAT ABOUT ROME!?*
Josey and I ask each other faux-defensively for days,
on the road, in our car, our rooms at Red Roof Inns.

*LOVE IT OR LEAVE IT!* We bray at each other, then laugh.
At the Red Roof Inns toilets wobble to and fro, or back and forth.
I dream I re-seat one of them, MacGyver everything up.

Dream-Josey says *you can do anything, even if you've only heard men
describe it just once and all wrong.* We are still thinking of that poor
white man, all the poor white men we meet on our tour of Slavery

in America, Generations of Enslavers, the Enslaved. White men
on these tours so hurt, so ready for us to be mad. At what?
I'm not mad at anybody who can keep their big mouth shut, but

*NOWADAYS WE EVEN GET UPSET ABOUT WATERBOARDING!*
this one needs to say next. Do we? I've lost track. *WE CAN'T
MAKE VALUE JUDGMENTS ABOUT THE PAST!* he blusters,

and I imagine smiling, chirping *Sure we can!*
He's a greatest-hits of all the guys we've met on all these tours:
Washington, Jefferson, Madison, a great white way

of enslavers. So I ask why it's important, why he needs us
to know slavery's always happened, and it's always passive
tense. I smile sweetly. I tell him I've been on a lot of these tours,

and the angry men who interrupt are always white, ask
if he knows why. But the gentleman loses his mind. White people
on the slavery tour, learning how many rapes it takes

to look white enough to pass, white enough
to say *I DON'T SEE WHAT RACE HAS TO DO
WITH ANYTHING* just once, and all wrong.

# You Are Her

Susan points
out whenever
you see a map
in the wild,
the map says *YOU*
*ARE HERE*
but everyone points
to the same spot, touches
the *E*, so it rubs off,
says *YOU ARE HER*.

You *are* her
when she says this: you
see it, you are Susan
in the wild, Susan
of the Plexi-covered
map, Susan at the O.K.
Corral. Susan seven, smirking
at Tomorrowland. Susan
at the Civic Center, Pike's
Peak, Baker Beach, Golden
Gate. At the liquid shift
of frazil ice thick

as lava below Lower
Yosemite Fall. You're
what's there, there
no longer there, visible
made invisible, *HERE*
now, *HER.*

# St. Ailred

Billy's eyes are tired, he's sick of this work.
There's no time for it's-not-fair, the almost-plea,
the best case scenario: an ex-good-kid in prison
the rest of his life, woman still dead, still shot

to death in her driveway. Billy, I am reading
about saints and relics, reliquaries, looking for
medallions online to keep you safe. St. Ailred's
the patron saint of integrity, known for his compassion,

clear writing. He's perfect for you, Billy. He's been dead
a thousand years. *Lives of the Scottish Saints* wants you to know
at his most sacred tomb the sick were cured, the lepers cleansed,
the wicked terrified, the blind received their sight.

# New Haven Sonnet

Every so often, often in fall, we remember
that public greens were once our burial grounds.
For hanged men, poxy corpses, the enslaved: the other,
from when the green was on the edge of town.
In New Haven, a headline reads "Skeleton Found
in Upended Tree on Green." With pictures of somebody's
skull in the root ball, Death Investigator down
in the pit fetching bones. Witnesses at the muddy
scene offer their views: *dead man trying to tell
a tale,* says one. The dog walker shouts *GIVE
A DOG A BONE!* Bones: just *an earthly shell,*
one lady shrugged. All here, all trying to live
with, reassure each other. We don't let the dead
*end up in the public works chipper,* a cop said.

# Oney Judge's New Shoes

"ABSCONDED from the household of the President of the United States, ONEY JUDGE, a light mulatto girl, much freckled, with very black eyes and bushy black hair, she is of middle stature, slender, and delicately formed, about 20 years of age."
—*The Philadelphia Gazette and Universal Daily Advertiser*, May 23, 1796

Here's what happened right before she left:
Washington gave her money for shoes. We still
have his accounts, the careful books he kept
of what he spent, on whom. Or what. She needed
new shoes, so she got the money, got to go
to the shoe guy, get a new pair made. Which she
would need for running off. But also the shoe guy,
a free Black preacher, was known for helping runaways.
I mean he was known by them. Not the enslavers.
He bought his own freedom with money he earned,
fighting in the revolution: total badass. Oney Judge
and Rev. Richard Allen, making her a pair of shoes:
Americans. The price of new shoes enough to buy
an hour out of the house, to make a plan with him.
Did he become a cobbler for this, for times like this?
He also worked as a chimney sweep, founded a whole
Church, the AME; nbd. I imagine the risk she took

to ask for more, scuffing over cobbled streets
to ruin what she had. What should we learn
to be what people need when they need us? To fix
what's wrong one chimney, one shoe at a time.

# Love and the Deli Counter

At my Stop & Shop the ladies at the deli counter
give us free slices of meat so we can talk about
how thin we want it. Everyone wants it thinner
but me. A woman asks for four slices shaved
ham. She can have anything she wants. I want
two pounds of turkey, sliced thick. I never
got the thin slice thing; it's hard to pick up. It tears.
It takes the ladies longer to cut it up. Here's what
I hate: inconveniencing ladies. One of the deli ladies
tells me the provolone piccante *smells like feet* and I
say *Way to sell it!* I make her coworker laugh,
which is all I want from a trip to the Stop & Shop.
She and I keep looking at each other, nodding as if
we are listening seriously while foot-taste cheese
lady makes her case; the foot taste is a good thing!
Then she wants to talk about not wearing socks
as a kid, getting in trouble with her mom. I love
them both. I am eating a free slice of turkey, thanking
them, telling another lady in the store I love the blue
and yellow grosgrain ribbon down her jeans' seams,
telling another *I love your boots.* There are no men
in the store. Saturday afternoon; we stroll the aisles,
kind to each other. Some days Boston is just a bunch

of women calling out to each other *I LOVE YOUR DRESS!*
We eat free turkey, help each other find the sour cream.
The checkout girl's name tag says *Love*. Love tells me
her mom called her *love* so much she just changed it.
I love it, love my Stop & Shop, her name, love
when people, strangers, call me *love* or *lovie*. At the gym
Christine says *Hello, love* until she learns my name;
a shame. At the deli counter, a woman dries her hands,
smiles at me, says *and what can I get you, my love?*

# Ken Chukwuba, Salt Lake City

I'm in Utah, which keeps surprising me.
Both Salt Lake City and me, here in it. Surprise:
they asked me to read at BYU, but said
swearing or saying "Jesus Christ" or "God"
wasn't okay. Or being gay. Okay. The gay
kiss-in in Temple Square. Surprise: we still do that.
Surprised each day by mountains taller than clouds,
than flight paths, freshly white each morning. Surprised
by all the white people, any Aryan crowd
making me look around, nervous. Surprise:
I don't like being white when everyone is,
and you can't always get coffee with your pie.
I went to rent a car downtown, surprised
the bus never came, surprised it took an hour
and a half to walk halfway. Surprised by the man
who rented me my car: Ken Chukwuba,
who feigned interest in me. "Why are you here?"
*I'm a visiting professor.* "That's good. Where
from?" *Boston.* He didn't look up, did paperwork.
"That's good. What do you teach?" *Poetry.* "That's good."
*Do you read poetry?* "No." *Then why
did you say* "that's good"? *You don't care.* Then Ken
Chukwuba started laughing, said if I

wrote him a poem I could keep the car
an extra day. Ken Chukwuba, I asked
how to say your name so I'd know where the stress
would fall. I teach people how to write in lines
of iambic pentameter, like what Shakespeare wrote,
but better. Because they write them in Salt Lake City,
in Utah, where the LDS stores grain
against the rapture in white silos, files
all our families' trees in mountain caves.
Because the inversion sometimes rises, clears
for Wasatch, Oquirrh, Timpanogos, Wolf,
and Ken Chukwuba and I are here.

# First Day

In law school, first day, in the movies, the prof says *Look*
*to the left of you. Look to your right. One of you*
*won't be here next year.* He's in a corduroy jacket, suede
elbows, picking out the girl he's going to fuck. My friend asks
if I do this first day of poetry school. Look here, I say: look
to the left of you look to the right look up look me over now reach.
Reach out, hold open your new friends' dear hands,
press your cheek to their knuckles, kiss their sweetly lined palms.
Really *look,* though, to the left and look over: Lord, overlook each
of us each of our faults. Keep looking, just *looking,* you know? Don't
stop. Look to your left on the Red Line; practice enchantment.
Pretend you're in love. Pretending enough you can feel this, fresh
tenderness for each, then all of the time. Look to your right, reach
your hand out: look like you're on acid, like you've never *seen*
a human hand before! What's the hand *feeling?* What's it like
to speak *Hand?* Look to the left of you, the hard right now. Look
forward, don't you ever look back. Except for with anger, or
something. Look back to take notes on what-all you sailed through,
and on the what-all you flunked. Look back on the sofa you puked
on: your mom picked that upholstery out. Your mom worked
so hard! Paid some off every week! You loved that old sofa,
its prim skirt or black bears. Its pink chintz, its velvet waterwheels.
So look back and look down and then look back in tears.

# Acknowledgments

These poems or earlier versions of them appeared in the following:

*The Adroit Journal:* "Ken Chukwuba, Salt Lake City"

*AGNI:* "Crying in the Cab Away from You" and "I Imagine the Butches'
Stripper Bar"

*Barely South Review:* "Heirloom"

*Bennington Review:* "Testicles at Trinity, the Atomic Testing Site"

*Bird's Thumb:* "Big Earth" and "A Decision Was Made"

*B O D Y:* "Poetry Class in a Massachusetts Prison"

*The Boston Globe:* "Backhoe in Snow, Boston"

*Broadsided:* "My History of Lead"

*Commonplace:* "Monticello Visit Sonnet"

*The Critical Flame:* "Lucky Ladies Sestina"

*The Dalhousie Review:* "First Day"

*The Drum:* "Horrors All Around"

*District Lit:* "Saint Ailred"

*The Gettysburg Review:* "Just Once and All Wrong" and "Putting the *Oh, Christ* Back in Christmas"

*Green Mountains Review:* "What a Waste" and "Missile and Space Gallery, National Museum of the U.S. Air Force"

*Hobart:* "Alone in Utah"

*Lambda Literary Review:* "You Are Her"

*Let the Bucket Down:* "Introductory Composition at a Massachusetts Prison," and "Poetry Class in a Massachusetts Prison"

*Literary Matters:* "Our Star"

*Malahat Review:* "Lucky Copper Smelter"

*Mapping Salt Lake City:* "Joe Hill's Prison"

*Memorious:* "Basic Writing Skills"

*Minnesota Review:* "New Haven Sonnet"

*Mortar Magazine:* "What We Can Imagine"

*Oxford American:* "Campsite, Shenandoah"

*Ploughshares:* "Why They Hate Us"

*Plume:* "Notnames at the Detroit Institute of Arts" and "Hell Fuckin' Yeah: SmackDown! vs. Raw"

*Poetry:* "Freedom" and "Donuts in Kidjail"

*Salamander:* "What Matters"

*Scoundrel Time:* "Spelling "Prostitutes'," "Rosa Parks Edits Her Statement as She Writes It," "A Cincinnati Stripper Bar," "The Serious Downer," and "On the Deerfield River"

*Southern Indiana Review:* "Reading 'What a Waste' to College Boys"

*Talking River Review:* "Free Will, Faith, and Fungus"

*The Common:* "Zero Slave Teeth"

*The Slowdown:* "I Imagine the Butches' Stripper Bar"

*The Threepenny Review:* "Dictionary Poem," "Path to Nowhere," and "What Kids Don't Know"

*Water~Stone Review:* "Sestina for the Women Locked Up in Framingham, Who Make American Flags"

*Writers Resist:* "Sonnet for Reading Aloud in Kidjail"

These poems were written with support from a Lannan Literary Fellowship, a Wallace Stegner Fellowship at Stanford University, the Dorothy and Lewis B. Cullman Center for Scholars and Writers at the New York Public Library, a Visiting Artist Residency at the American Academy in Rome, a Visiting Writer position at Westminster College, and a Joseph P. Healey Research Grant and Dean's Research Funds from the University of Massachusetts Boston. Thank you.

# Recent Titles from Alice James Books

Alice James Books is committed to publishing books that matter. The press was founded in 1973 in Boston, Massachusetts as a cooperative, wherein authors performed the day-to-day undertakings of the press. This element remains present today, as authors who publish with the press are invited to collaborate closely in the publication process of their work. AJB remains committed to its founders' original feminist mission, while expanding upon the scope to include all voices and poets who might otherwise go unheard. In keeping with its efforts to build equity and increase inclusivity in publishing and the literary arts, AJB seeks out poets whose writing possesses the range, depth, and ability to cultivate empathy in our world and to dynamically push against silence. The press was named for Alice James, sister to William and Henry, whose extraordinary gift for writing went unrecognized during her lifetime.

Designed by Pamela A. Consolazio

*Spark design*

Printed by McNaughton & Gunn

## *STORYBOOK ND*

CURATED BY GINI ALHADEFF

César Aira, *The Famous Magician*

Osamu Dazai, *Early Light*

Helen DeWitt, *The English Understand Wool*

László Krasznahorkai, *Spadework for a Palace*

Clarice Lispector, *The Woman Who Killed the Fish*

Yoko Tawada, *Three Streets*

## *FORTHCOMING*

Natalia Ginzburg, *The Road to the City*

Rachel Ingalls, *In the Act*

# THE FAMOUS MAGICIAN
## CÉSAR AIRA

translated from the Spanish
by Chris Andrews

STORYBOOK ND

Originally published in Spanish as *El ilustre mago*
Published by arrangement with Literarische Agentur Michael Gaeb, Berlin

Manufactured in the United States of America
First published clothbound by New Directions in 2022

*Library of Congress Cataloging-in-Publication Data*
Names: Aira, César, 1949– author. | Andrews, Chris, 1962– translator.
Title: The famous magician / César Aira ; translated from the Spanish by Chris Andrews.
Other titles: Ilustre mago. English
Description: First edition. | New York : New Directions Books, 2020. | "Originally published in Spanish as El ilustre mago"—Title page verso.
Identifiers: LCCN 2020012676 | ISBN 9780811228893 (hardcover ; acid-free paper) | ISBN 9780811228909 (ebook)
Classification: LCC PQ7798.1.I7 I4813 2020 | DDC 863/.64—dc23
LC record available at https://lccn.loc.gov/2020012676

10 9 8 7 6 5 4 3 2 1

New Directions Books are published for James Laughlin
by New Directions Publishing Corporation
80 Eighth Avenue, NY 10011

# THE FAMOUS MAGICIAN

One Sunday morning, when I had already passed the age of sixty and come to enjoy a certain renown as a writer, I was strolling through the book market in Parque Rivadavia, not looking for anything in particular, just enjoying the sunshine, with no pressing tasks to fulfill or problems weighing on my mind. The sky was blue, the birds were singing, and the few trees left standing stood very still, as if frightened, each leaf precisely etched against the air. When I lowered my gaze to the earth and examined the labyrinth of green metal book stands, I could see, through the gaps, in the park beyond, the havoc wrought by the storm of the night before. Hundred-year-old trees lay strewn, piled one on top of the other, their branches and foliage promiscuously tangled, exhibiting roots that looked like gross earthen sculptures of spiders and squids. Likewise, the iron park benches had been thrown into heaps of up to twenty, twisted out of shape and mangled together by the power of the storm. Even the marble and bronze statues had been blown off their pedestals, no doubt all at once by an irresistible gust, and they must have crashed together in midair, to judge from the resulting blend of body parts: the breasts of a Venus plus the legs of a horse with the three-cornered hat of a founding father, and other such weird chimeras half-buried in

7

hillocks of mashed-up lawn. I heard one of the book-sellers saying that the people living in the buildings that faced the park had filmed those apocalyptic dances and were uploading them to their Facebook pages, using video editing software to insert rabbits and ducks on the pretext that those little white figures would serve as points of reference.

None of this was of much interest to me. My Sunday walk through the market, repeated over so many years, was part of my general fantasizing about books. The multiplying titles opened up a wealth of creative paths, and though I knew I wouldn't follow even one of them, their mere existence comforted me. I sometimes felt that I'd already read too much, and had exhausted the store of books that I really wanted to read. But the desire to read was still there in me, and it was as if that desire were engendering new books, no less desirable for being nonexistent. Something similar was happening with my writing. I didn't want to know what my as-yet-unwritten books would be about; I wanted them to emerge from reality, like a clown on a spring jumping out of a box, rather than from my thoughts. But the problem was nothing was jumping. I hadn't been able to write for some time: the tributaries that nourished my inspiration were starting to run dry. And without those tributaries, all I'd have was the central current of my life, which I had striven so hard to keep secret. I had invested all my spiritual riches in the elaboration of screen memories, and exploiting them to go on writing was the last thing I wanted to do. The storms of life had left painful scars—I wanted to forget. I had no idea that oblivion was tensing its muscles, preparing to attack.

Which it did, as I was leaving that labyrinth of bookstalls, in the form of a character I would rather not have seen. He was one of the dying breed of old hands, displaced by young dealers of pirated movies and games. The real booksellers had left years before. Just a few had hung on from the golden age, and the residue of that residue was the individual in question. He was basically down and out, but had intellectual pretensions. He had been a vendor once, before the municipal authorities set up the new stalls and began to issue formal permits. I was vaguely aware that he had a history of drug use, violence, and all sorts of problems. I had never inquired into the details, not for lack of curiosity but because I never talked with anyone in the park ... except for him, and what he gave me, naturally, was the expurgated version. I knew that if he saw me, he wouldn't let me get away. Which made me keep an eye out for him, and avoid the places where he liked to hang around. He was a fat, scruffy man, somewhere between forty and fifty, his hair and beard forming a single shaggy mass that almost hid a pale, puffy, girlish face with pursed lips, uniformly rotten teeth, and bloodshot eyes. He had a wobbling gait, and the pauses in his speech conveyed the smug assurance of a man supremely full of himself. Conceit was never less justified. How he survived was a mystery. But people like that always get by somehow, making those of us who work and lead orderly middle-class lives feel stupid. His name was Ovando. I had known that since the day, years before, when he had given me a copy of his only book, in a shoddy, self-published edition. It was supposed to be a novel, apparently. I couldn't read more than a few pages; it was too awful. I know it shouldn't bother me, but I always find such cases depressing. I have never been able to understand how there can be bad writers. All the elements required for writing well are right there in Literature, served up on a silver platter. I can't see the flaw in this reasoning, however I look at it, and yet overwhelming empirical evidence contradicts it.

On this occasion, Ovando said straight away that he had an important proposal to make. I was still thinking that if I had turned left to go out onto the avenue instead of turning right, I would have avoided him, but reality was defeating me. When I took in his words, I nodded and half smiled as if to say, "I'll hear you out, with all the sympathy and attention I can muster, but I don't think I'll accept any part of what you're proposing, because at my age, and in my current state of semi-retirement, I systematically avoid committing myself to projects that—no matter how well-intentioned the people who put them forward may be—always mean extra work to do." It might seem excessive to claim that a slight inclination of the head and the contraction of a few secondary muscles around the mouth can transmit such a long and nuanced message, but really there's nothing strange about that at all. More can be said with even less, if the context is taken into account. In this case, the hint was lost on my interlocutor.

"You and I need to have a quiet talk. Let's go to the café over there."

Against all my principles, I let him drag me along. Weakness of character, malleability of will, misplaced politeness: all these faults, of which I was, I knew, a living catalog, might however have had some benefits in the end, because they resulted in problems that I would have avoided otherwise, and the sum (or the remainder) of those problems was all there had ever been of reality in my life. The cars on the avenue nearly killed us, but didn't. I felt I was acting under duress, walking across the hot asphalt beside that heaving, panting creature. We reached the sidewalk on the other side and entered The Collector. It was full, but Ovando wove his way in, greeting people here and there (he claimed to know everyone involved in small-time trafficking of stamps and coins), and managed to find a table where we were extremely uncomfortable, wedged in among the philatelists.

He started telling me, in rather vague terms, about various suburban mysteries. There was something about the Calle Cachimayo, supposedly paved with philosophers' stones, and a sect that was brainwashing the municipal councilors, and Literature. Maybe all three were somehow related. It sounded insubstantial. But it might have been my fault, since I wasn't paying much attention. In my spiritual development, I had graduated from that kind of material. Or to be more precise, I had built it into my work with a fantastic twist. Ovando went on, completely oblivious to my lack of interest. Paradoxically, charlatans of his kind are always talking earnestly about the progress they've made in perceiving the subtlest vibrations of thought exactly when they're failing to realize how profoundly they are boring their listeners.

He finally succeeded in jolting me out of my torpor when he told me that he could bend the laws of physics to his will and compel them to do his bidding. I took this to be a purely verbal declaration and replied accordingly: I said that we all have that power, which is granted to us along with our material existence. Now it was my turn to get his attention; I had actually disconcerted him.

"What," he asked in a threatening tone of voice, "do you mean?"

"Well ... if I drop this spoon"—I took the coffee spoon from my saucer and held it delicately between thumb and forefinger, level with my head—"it will fall to the ground, which is what I want it to do, so I will have succeeded in commanding the law of gravity to obey me."

"Very clever," he said, barely stifling his rage. "But I also said, *if* you were listening, that I can *bend* those laws any way I like. Do you think everyone can do that?"

I improvised a response, just for the fun of it:

"If I tie the spoon to my hand with a thread, it won't hit the ground when I drop it, so I will have fooled the law of gravity."

He didn't bother to compliment me on my ingenuity. He looked pointedly at the spoon that I was still holding up in the air.

"Drop it."

I did, and to my enormous surprise, the little silvery object fell to within half an inch of the floor, then, as Ovando said "Jump, Gyp," flew back up to my hand.

I looked around: my immediate reaction was naturally to worry that we might have attracted attention. But no one had noticed. The stamp collectors were totally focused on the specimens that they were exchanging, as if a moment's distraction might have been enough to disperse their collections. I thought I had misheard, which would not have been unlikely, given the racket reigning supreme, and the café's maddening acoustics. Arguing fiercely, the stamp and coin collectors were all talking at the same time, at the top of their voices; it sounded as if they were about to come to blows, but that was just an effect of their fervor. The continuous jingling sound of the drachmas and the obols, audible beneath the shouting, might have been mistaken for the chirping of caged mechanical birds. Then I realized my mistake: it was true that the racket was driving me crazy, and I couldn't lip-read, but I hadn't *heard* that jumping spoon; I had seen it.

From that point on, I began to take Ovando seriously. Which is not to say that I was paying more attention to what he was saying. I couldn't; there was too much to think about. I was mentally reconstructing what he had told me: it had gone in one ear and out the other, as I said, on the assumption that it was nothing but the chatter of a gullible fool, and yet it had clearly left a trace, an impression, in reverse perhaps, as when a stamp is applied to a virgin surface (like my brain): with a little effort, reversing the trace, I felt I might decipher it. What he had been proposing, I deduced, was that I join forces with him in order to achieve total control of power, although that sounds like a pleonasm. On his own, he had only been able to reach a certain point. To go any further, he would need the help of the Fairy Literature and her gifts. But why me? I didn't want to delude myself into thinking that my style was the key to the secrets of the Universe. It was more likely that I was the only writer he knew, or knew well enough to involve in his scheme. His opening moves had deeply unsettled me. But on another plane of my consciousness, I was already building barricades of disbelief. Although I don't want to blow my own horn, I should mention that I am an intellectual as well as a writer. Cartesian reasoning works in me independently of my will, even if in my case it is contaminated by literary experiences, colored and enriched by flashes of imagination. That must have been what he wanted me for: his powers, if he really had any, needed to be channeled rationally.

He had gone on talking, and I had to force myself to listen. He was demanding an exclusive commitment. Did that mean I wouldn't be able to write? Precisely.

"And what about reading?" I asked.

He had already moved on to something else; the remark about exclusive commitment had been made some minutes earlier, so he had to rewind, with some help from me. His reply was firm:

"In general, I advise against reading: it's a waste of

time and dangerous for the purity of the soul. In your case, once you begin your study of these mysteries, you'll have to completely forego that harmful activity."

"But I couldn't live without reading. Life would be too boring."

"You won't be bored, believe me."

We chatted on like that for a while. All very hypothetical, but I found the topic amusing. I asked him if he had other powers, apart from making spoons disobey the law of gravity.

"All the powers that Magic grants. I can pass from life to death and back, make my organs dance the rumba, shift objects and living beings by the power of thought, transform matter, etcetera. And when I say etcetera, it's not just a figure of speech."

"You don't think you might be exaggerating?"

"I could give you proof, but that would be rather puerile."

"Yes, of course. Anyway, proof doesn't prove anything."

"What do you mean?!"

"Proof can always be faked."

"Not if it's real proof."

I wasn't convinced. I was still on the plane of harmless abstractions, in spite of the spoon. One of the things he had said was that my reward for becoming his associate would be to share all his magical powers: that had set me daydreaming.

Clearly running out of patience, he told me to pay attention. He picked up a sugar cube, put it on the palm of his hand, which was puffed up like a boxing glove, and stared intently at the small white block, which began to tremble and make little movements, as if unsuccessfully trying to escape. Yielding no doubt to the suggestive power of the situation, I imagined that the cube was alarmed at the prospect of losing its nature as sugar. But the transmutation had already begun: one grain after another took on a golden glow, and in seconds the whole cube was solid gold, with a slightly granular surface; its form had remained exactly the same. Ovando put it on the table and invited me to examine it. Although I know nothing about metals, as soon as I picked it up I could tell it was the finest gold, thanks to an intuition that must have been speaking to me from the ages of myth, and speaking truly, I was sure of that.

When I looked up, the man sitting opposite seemed to have been transformed as well. He was still the same scruffy hustler I had come into the café with, but now I saw him as the magician that he had proved himself to be, surrounded by an aura of power. My feelings at that moment were contradictory. I admired and almost venerated him for having achieved such mastery, but it was not a disinterested admiration since I couldn't help longing to possess that power myself, and a painful sense of impotence, frustration or even fatality was rising from the depths of my soul. Like all timid people, I had fantasized about omnipotence since childhood (what else could I have dreamed of or desired?). The consoling power of those fantasies depended on the certitude that omnipotence was not of this world. Seeing it in action, right before my eyes in the banal setting of a café, which made the proof all the more conclusive, threw me into anguished doubts about reality itself.

I was on the point of accepting his conditions and asking when we would start. But I restrained myself. He had said that I would have to trust him implicitly and follow his instructions for years, accompanying him on his intergalactic voyages. Reacting against my initial impulse, I went to the other extreme and told myself that all this was impossible. Such things don't happen in reality. And yet ... that was precisely the point: to outwit reality itself. Still, giving up writing and reading, abandoning my work and my books, would leave me without any consolation. It would be like giving up life itself. On the other hand, I couldn't help imagining all I could do with the powers that he was offering me. Giving up Literature was a terrible wrench; moments before, it had seemed unthinkable, and I still couldn't really envisage it. And yet what was Literature, what had it been for me if not the protean power of transformation, which I now had the means to transpose to the plane of reality? From that point of view, I wouldn't be abandoning Literature so much as transcending it. I had often spoken and written of "abandon," taking Rimbaud in Africa as my model. Considering my readers, wouldn't it be a nice gesture on my part to follow suit in reality? Reality: that was the source of my torment. Something that I had treated as a literary theme was happening in *reality*, to me. Could I let this opportunity pass? Yes, of course I could. I knew myself well enough to know that my cowardice was capable of that, and of much more besides.

"It's a difficult decision."

"I know."

"Do I have to give you an answer right away?"

"No, but I can't wait long. A week, not one day more. Meet me here next Sunday at the same time."

He was about to get up.

I asked:

"Can I keep the cube of ... gold?"

With a largesse I wouldn't have thought him capable of displaying, he simply smiled and left.

This was the beginning of a period of reflection or decision-making, but I suspect that I failed to distinguish between the two processes: a serious error, since in my case they are totally opposed. First I had to finish assimilating the incident. That was the most difficult thing. How can you assimilate the unassimilable? On the evidence of what I had seen (and of what, above all, I was carrying in my pocket), the man was a formidable magician ... Ovando, of all people! For years I had been seeing him in the park on Sunday and always taken him for one of those losers who hover around the second-hand book trade, semiemployed and scraping by, readers of Hermann Hesse and Camus ... That's what he was, no doubt about it. And yet, while I had been writing my books and becoming a distinguished author, he had been acquiring the knowledge and power with which to make me leave my books behind. With a diabolical acumen, he had intuited how to tempt me. I had always thought that only one thing could persuade me to stop writing and reading: the offer of a vast sum of money, an inexhaustible bank account. Nothing else would do it—and yet there was something else. Something I had failed to take into account because it had no place in reality. But reality is limited, like everything that has a name. The same is true of the Universe itself, the All. And there lay the power of Magic, which I had so often toyed with in my novels. The proposal had come at just the right moment. I had outgrown the fantasy of exchanging Literature for wealth. Now that I had reached my sixties, the modest amount of money at my disposal was more than I could spend, and other priorities had emerged, such as health. A series of dislocations had left me in a bad way. And from what I had gathered about my unexpected Mephistopheles, the powers that he was offering to share with me included absolute control over one's body.

I still couldn't believe it, of course. Although, in a way, I did, if only hypothetically. As so often before, I had a backup: what I didn't actually do, I could still write about. Everything was grist to the mill of storytelling. A person appearing like a genie from a lamp to offer me magic powers in exchange for a renunciation: it was like something from a tale, not something that might really happen. But didn't the Literature that I would have to renounce belong to that same realm of dreams? If proof was required, then none was better than the fact that I had always written about Magic.

And yet that commonality was ultimately what separated Magic and Literature in the most categorical way. The renunciation that Ovando the Magician was asking of me made sense. The two things were incompatible. From childhood (or almost), I had thought of myself as a writer and never as anything else, but perhaps that was simply an effect of inattention. Perhaps the moment had come to see things clearly. Vocations are about becoming rather than being, and if, as I believed, I had become a writer, why go on? What was left for me to do? Repeat what I had done, like a shadow of my former self, itself a shadow of what I should have been, prolonging a decadence that, paradoxically, was costing me more and more effort, ever greater struggles to overcome my growing disinclination? Also, what I had always disliked about my work as a storyteller was the dull, gray time that had to be spent laboriously writing it all out, scene after scene, paragraph after paragraph, sweating away like Sisyphus to fill up the hundred or so pages required to make a book. And in response to that familiar complaint, a possibility had sprung from nowhere—an offer of magical instantaneity. But the possibility (once again, the seesaw of my indecision was tilting back the other way, pursuing its mad dance) existed only outside Literature.

This dilemma occupied my thoughts without respite. I couldn't say how many times I turned it over in my mind, weighing up the pros and cons. In the end I did the sane thing and gave up. I wasn't going to be able to solve the problem on my own, so I decided to seek advice, disinterested or not. I would do what I had so often done: let others decide for me. But as I had also so often done, I procrastinated. A week is not much time, but it's enough to let things slide from one day to the next, so Friday came around before I had confided in anyone. What I did in the meantime was go to one of those gold dens on Calle Libertad and have the cube assayed. The jeweler was not in the least surprised by the form of the object; he must have been accustomed to the inexplicable. He did the test and told me that it was gold of the highest purity; he could offer me twelve hundred pesos. I replied that, for the moment, I didn't want to sell it. I went away thinking how paradoxical it was that magical, alchemical, mystical gold could become (and there, precisely, resided all the magic, the alchemy, and the mystery) common, ordinary gold, of the kind that is tested and weighed and valued. It felt as if it had undergone a second transformation.

As I said, Friday came, and not only had I not made a decision, I hadn't asked anyone for advice. But mentally at least I hadn't been entirely idle: during that week, I considered each thing I did and every step I took in the light of the choice that I was facing. And I believe that I saw things as I had never seen them before: thrown into relief by the radical possibility that life as I had known it might cease forever. And I wondered if that life—the dull daily routine of a petit-bourgeois conformist, repeated without variation for decades—could really be too high a price to pay for the most extraordinary adventure that

I would ever have the chance to embark upon. Though it's not really fair to present it like that, since actual lives never have the glamour of the lives that might have been.

Anyway, first thing on Friday, I got onto my old bike and rode to San Telmo to have lunch with Ernesto, having decided to tell him the whole story and ask for his advice. I knew in advance that his exquisite English courtesy would prevent him from doing anything so vulgar as actually advising me, but I also knew that a conversation with an intelligent liberal can be extremely enlightening. On the way, as I pedaled along completely absorbed in my thoughts—saved by Providence alone from being run over by a car or riding into the path of an oncoming bus—I rehearsed my explanation. I foresaw that Ernesto, well-read skeptic that he was, would find it hard to believe the fantastic story that I was about to tell. I could see it from his point of view; I would have had the same reaction. I was convinced, but only because I had seen and touched the proof, and I could offer no proof to Ernesto, only my word, which, incidentally, was all that I had ever been able to offer anyone. But the obstacle was not insuperable, because I could present the problem as a hypothetical case, or as the plot of a novel.

A little while later, there he was, sitting across the table from me in the café on the corner of Perú and México, cheerful and chatty, talking about the books that he had just bought and what he was reading, as he had done so often in our conversations over the years.

Readers seek out fellow readers as much as they seek out books, though fellow readers are, alas, more difficult to find. So we hold onto them for life. Ernesto was my reading master; he had introduced me to many of the authors I had ended up plagiarizing—Gobineau, for example.

On this occasion, however, our usual topic was deferred.

"Something strange has happened to me," I said, "the strangest thing that could ever have happened, all because I met a magician with the most incredible powers." I proceeded to give him an exhaustive account of my conversation with Ovando in The Collector, complete with all the details so as to make it clear that there had been no trickery or sleight of hand behind the proof that I had witnessed. He listened without showing any sign of incredulity or modifying even for a moment his attentive and polite expression. When I finished, he raised his eyebrows, as if to say: Is that all? No, of course it wasn't all; I had left out the most important part, the reason why I had told him the story: "This magician has offered to make me his partner (please don't laugh, I'm deadly serious) and show me how to acquire those powers. But first I'll have to give up Literature, that marvelous triviality. And that's the dilemma I'm facing now, because he's given me a deadline, and I've only got two days left to make up my mind."

It's funny how a story changes according to the listener. Ernesto's personality, so masterful in spite (or because) of his British aloofness, gave my little story a humorous overtone, transformed it into a piece of ironic orientialism. I had asked him not to laugh, and he didn't. His body language suggested that he was about to administer a lesson, but I couldn't imagine what it might be. I would not have been at all upset had he scoffed at my childishness, not only because of the friendship that bound us, but also because, in accordance with the strict moral code of his masters, he held immaturity in the highest esteem, and credited it with creative powers of which I was less convinced.

He asked me about the Magician himself; I had been a little vague on that score. Not wishing to hide anything, I said who he was. Ernesto knew him:

"He's a charlatan, a sycophant. I often see him hanging around second-hand bookstores, looking for some innocent soul to involve in his shady deals or bore with his conversation, at least. This must be some new story that he's pulled out of his hat, dreamed up specially for you, I would guess. If I can give you some friendly advice: forget the whole thing, or use it as a plot for a novel. It's like what happened to Pessoa with Aleister Crowley. Or it's just a shell game, where people try to guess which shell or cup the marble is hidden under— they never win, as I'm sure you know, because the illusionist places the marble *after* his victim has made a choice."

His example gave me an idea:

"Wouldn't it be interesting to write about someone who had a sort of second-degree naivety? A hick comes to the city and sees one of those swindlers winning piles of money. He doesn't realize it's a scam; he thinks that's just how it works. He has heard people saying that "the house always wins," so it occurs to him that this could be a good little earner. He gets three coffee cups and a marble, and sets himself up in Plaza Once. Heh heh, what a fool. The only person in the history of humanity ever to play the game honestly. Not because he's honest but because he's a naive provincial. The people who lay bets in this game are completely naive themselves; but by choosing to lay their bets with our hick, they automatically cease to be prey, and become almost predatory, without meaning to, out of sheer naivety! From there, it can go a number of ways—"

Ernesto interrupted me:

"I assure you that this magician of yours is not naive; he's not playing straight, not even unintentionally."

"The analogy doesn't work anyhow, because what he showed me wasn't a trick."

"I didn't say it was. But what is authentic is not always best. Authenticity can be false too."

"So you think it's trivial to turn a sugar cube into gold? If that's not Magic ..."

"Yes, I think it's trivial, vulgar, and banal. I'm sorry."

It was like one of his literary judgements, and I felt that we were still talking at cross purposes. It would certainly be vulgar and banal for a magician like Ovando to appear in a faux-oriental tale and offer to pass on his powers to a disciple, and all the rest. But in reality?

Before I could voice this objection, he was refuting it triumphantly. Heaving the sort of sigh that we reserve for dealing with incorrigible children, he asked me to pay attention.

He put his hand on the book that I had laid on the table, a well-thumbed old copy of *Don Segundo Sombra*. Between his fingers, I saw its form and color change. When he took his hand away, it had turned into *Nouvelles impressions d'Afrique*, a first edition, uncut. Leafing through it with reverent admiration gave me time to start calming the welter of contradictions that were swirling around in my brain.

"I didn't know that you ..."

"Me and everyone else."

"Except me."

All he did was smile. For the first time in my life I felt that my inferiority complex was justified. "You think these powers are of little value, but I'm afraid I don't agree. On the contrary, they're enormously valuable to me, and if I'm hesitating about the offer, it's because the price I have to pay is enormous too."

"You said he would forbid you to read?"

"He says it's a harmful activity."

"Of course it is! That's why we cherish it."

He never missed an opportunity to indulge his fondness for paradoxes. And that was just the opening of the speech that he then delivered, advising me against embarking on a partnership with the Magician. My account of it will be rough and ready, since I can't hope to reproduce the elegant concision of his sentences. Basically, it was a hymn to reading and a demonstration of its superiority to Magic. Magic, he said, was very limited, limited to itself: it was what it was and nothing more. Admittedly, Magic could do anything: move objects, transform them, make them appear or disappear, but always on the condition that it remained itself, the same old Magic condemned to go on reusing its stale old power. Reading, on the other hand, was always going beyond itself, because it had nothing of its own; it had what it had provisionally, on loan from the book, which kept changing. Reading's paradoxical weapon was passivity ("and don't give me that macho nonsense about the active, creative, or vengeful reader"), surrender to a higher objectivity—that is, to the book. In a growing library that objectivity was manifest as the Magic of Magics, including all the others as effects. Magic properly so called was barely a cause, orphaned and astray.

I was unconvinced and justifiably, I think. I was given to that sort of reasoning myself; I kept filling my books with it, which, incidentally, was why they were so unattractive to readers. In my case it was all about euphony, sentences that sounded good, to my ear at least; I wasn't committed to their meanings. Ernesto chose his words more responsibly, but I couldn't help hearing them as if they had come out of my mouth.

On the way home I was thinking that I hadn't made any progress. What new knowledge I had gained was balanced by new ignorance, which confirmed the epistemological rule: we only ask questions to which we already have the answers. Knowing Ernesto, what else could I have expected him to say?

Although I was preoccupied by these thoughts, the long ride back to Flores was exerting pressure on my senses. It was a state that I knew well: the ecstasy of the real. I was feeling that ecstasy vicariously, as discourse, but enjoying it fully even so, given my cast of mind. I had regarded it up until then as a complement to my engagement with Literature, from which it may have been derived. But the time could well have come for reality to declare its independence from my dreams. Perhaps something new was beginning for me, after a lifetime spent among books: a superior kind of reading, the reading of the real world. I knew what Ernesto would have said to this (because I had continued our conversation in his absence, as I pedaled from block to block): he would have said that reality, like the magic it obeyed, was a single entity, locked up in the jail of itself, which it had built in order to be real. I brushed this sophistry aside, along with a passing thought, provoked by a twinge in my arm from a recent dislocation: the thought that, with the powers I was about to acquire, these minor pains and underlying fears about the frailty of my body would cease ... That notion was selfish and secondary: the Magician hadn't chosen me so I could recover from my dislocations but rather to help him solve the ultimate mysteries of the Universe.

Reality was prevailing, just as the bicycle was prevailing over distance. It was as if I were headed not for my home in Flores, but for the dawn-inhabited deserts, the mountains in the sky, the jungles, where everything is possible.

Evanescent as mist, my enthusiasm dissipated as I took a shower. Not knowing what to do, I watched a movie on television, then prepared something for dinner, and strange as it may sound took a nap. What better way to welcome a prodigious destiny than with a plunge into sleep's deep waters? I reemerged with my mind in turmoil, unable to tell circles from squares, up from down, black from white. It was my megalomania that had allowed me to accept being treated like a child by all the people who knew me well—they were the ones who had let my head swell, by overpraising my juvenilia. But submitting to so much condescension had ended up convincing me, in the inner sanctum of my unconscious, that I was still young. It didn't seem incongruous to me to be venturing into the supernatural when—given my age—what I should have been doing was taking my grandchildren to the park.

Once, only once, I had, in my green youth, tried to practice a mystical art, and failed. I had heard of a method for withstanding the cold. Apparently certain Tibetan lamas are able to live in the mountains, in subzero temperatures, wearing only light cotton tunics, thanks to a method of mobilizing all the body's internal organs. I was fervently determined to follow their example. For the highly imaginative young man that I was, it might seem a failure of imagination to aspire to no greater magical feat than remaining indifferent to the cold in spite of being lightly dressed. On the contrary, that choice was, I believe, a genuine imaginative triumph. So much so, in fact, that I have never since attempted any kind of personal transformation in real life, only in Literature.

I got up, refreshed by my nap, ready for acts of unheard-of audacity, as if there were nothing I could not do. Little by little the choice that I still had to make came back into my mind. I have to confess that my view of it was colored by an idea. I suspect that deep down I was hatching the thoroughly deceitful scheme of playing along with the Magician in order to gather material for my writing. That would have made sense, because for some time I had been exploring all the byways of invention and experience in the hope of reinventing myself, or if that proved impossible, at least emerging from a long period of sterility. And the subject matter that held out the possibility of renewal—Magic—had been my favorite of late. All my other themes had been drifting in that direction: a natural drift for a writer, perhaps, or at least for the sort of writer who, like me, has tired of life.

And to think I had always wanted to write adventure stories! Magic is the opposite of adventure, its perfect inversion. Even so, magical operations could have produced good literary results (as they had in former times) if not for a technical defect that rendered them unacceptable in our age of sophistication: they required the mechanical repetition of certain episodes, which can work in popular storytelling but not in high culture. This had been borne home to me by the events of that very morning: Ernesto's performance had been a mechanical and therefore completely predictable repetition of what the obese Magician had done the previous

Sunday. That didn't make the feat any less surprising in reality, but if I was going to put it in a story, I would have to add labored variations, which none of my readers would find convincing.

Of course, if I accepted the challenge, I wouldn't be writing stories. I would never write anything again, which suddenly made me feel very free in relation to the facts. Initially, giving up Literature had seemed apocalyptic but maybe it wasn't so terrible after all.

These reflections, which might have been taken from a handbook for writing workshops, seemed—with my future at stake—out of place and trivial, but they turned out to be relevant later on, when I visited my publisher Francisco at his bookstore. He can't have been expecting me because I never go out on a Friday afternoon when traffic's at its worst, and Buenos Aires becomes impossible. But I had no choice on this occasion, because the store isn't open on Saturdays: once again I was cursing myself for being such a procrastinator. It took me about an hour to get there in a taxi, when on any other day of the week it would have been a twenty-minute trip at most. (And it would be worse on the way back.)

All the same, I arrived before the regulars who drop in every afternoon. Francisco was at the computer, while Nico, his assistant, was arranging books on the shelves. The welcome was warm, as always. We went to the back room and sat down. Just that once, I said yes to a whiskey. Francisco showed me the new books on his list, fresh from the printer. So often, in the past, there had been one of mine in the batch ... The sad thought that perhaps I would publish no more books prevented me from really paying attention. I couldn't reply coherently to several of Francisco's questions—I was too distracted—and the conversation would have gone on flagging if I hadn't cut to the chase. I gathered my courage and told him the whole story.

"I don't believe," Francisco said, when I had finished, "that you could stop writing."

"Well, I could," I said emphatically. "In fact, I think I could do it even without embarking on this new mystical career. For the last few years, I've been 'marking time,' writing out of habit, because it's the only thing I know how to do, not because I really believe that I'm going to produce anything good."

Francisco brushed my assertions aside with a solid argument: I had been saying the same thing for twenty years and I was still writing.

"The pitcher goes to the well until ..."

To my surprise, he changed the subject: he asked me about a French author, and then about a book of conversations with John Baldessari, and various other things. Somewhat timidly, I returned to my theme:

"Do you think I should accept?"

It took him a moment to react. Accept what? That translation of Raymond Roussel that I had been asked to do? The invitation to Russia? Ah, no, that business with the fat guy from Parque Rivadavia.

"Come on, César! I thought it was a plot for a novel ..."
He was kidding me, but I pretended not to have noticed.

"It's perfectly real; it happened just like I told you. You know I never talk about my ideas for stories; if I did, I'd lose the desire to write them. It's a rule I adopted many years ago after spoiling lots of good ideas, and now I respect it scrupulously. By the way, that guarantees I'm telling the truth: I write everything I dream up, so if I *tell* people something, it means it really happened; it's not something I imagined. If it's the fruit of my imagination, my lips are sealed: I keep it for writing."

"All the same, that encounter in Parque Rivadavia is better as something imagined than as something that really occurred. As a real event, it's very banal."

"You think it's banal to flout the laws of physiology and physics?"

"Yes, totally banal. Those laws are dead letters. Haven't you ever heard the saying 'every law has its loophole?'"

"I think that refers to a different kind of law."

"A law's a law. Look." Francisco picked up a chewed pencil stub that was lying on the coffee table and rubbed it gently between his index finger and his thumb. I saw its shape and size change, until it became a Montblanc Bohème with a platinum nib. He must have guessed that I'd been coveting that pen for years.

I felt like a toy manipulated by grand masters of the art of living. I had never lived. All I had done was read and write, and I had believed the handful of readers who had seen that as some kind of privilege, but it was all a simulacrum of real life, a convenient substitute, even if

33

it had spared me many problems. All the things that had happened to me, from the most real (my dislocations) to the most unreal (my infantile fantasies of wealth), were tangled up in a Gordian knot of indecision.

Francisco had changed the subject again. He was talking about a book of mine that was about to come out, and others that were soon to be republished ... As if what I had told him and what he had just done were matters of no importance, and clearly, for him, that was the case. Was I making a mountain out of a molehill? Noticing how wretched I looked, he seemed to take pity on me.

"Look, if it's any help, my advice is to forget all about this unfortunate episode, which seems to have really shaken you up, and get on with your writing. The poetry in your books, *blah blah blah* ..."

I won't transcribe what he said. Not that I'm averse to praise, which always works like a welcome balm on my chronic insecurity. But it would cheapen Francisco's compliments to reproduce them with my pen; I leave them to the reader's obliging imagination. The idea, in short, was that "the poetry in my books" was a form of freedom, without which I wouldn't be able to live. Implacably confined by Magic, I would be stripped of that freedom. Magic, underneath its tinsel, was a mechanism like any other. It seemed to be an accumulation of causes without effects, but it was the cause, unique and implacable. Its multiplicity was an illusion, a time-honored error. Whereas the humble art of poetry (which I practiced, according to Francisco), by not laying claim to anything real behind or beyond the words, created true realities that were airy, light, protean, iridescent ... Also, he said—descending from those sublime flights of rhetoric only to rebound and soar higher still—also, there were the readers I had fashioned and educated; I had to think of them.

Apart from this last remark, which failed to penetrate my thick shell of bitterness, Francisco's arguments were ideally chosen to persuade me. Not only because they were good (which could in any case be disputed), but also because they were mine. I was amazed to find him saying what I thought, in my own words. Could he have been reproducing something that I had written or said somewhere? I couldn't remember having laid it all out so clearly. It was as if I had put the words into Francisco's mouth. Perhaps the same thing had happened with his demonstration of supernatural powers. Perhaps it was in the very nature of Literature that everyone should have such powers, except for the writer, defined as such precisely by that lack. Naturally, everyone else would encourage the writer to go on writing, so as not to lose the powers they enjoyed.

With the best of intentions, my friends had shown me that magical powers weren't so special. They had them, and could have used them to exploit my ignorance to their advantage. I should have been grateful: they had made a considerable sacrifice by laying their cards on the table. But the essential part of their lesson had failed to convince me: they were trying to show me that Literature was superior to Magic, and although I could see the relevance of their arguments, I still had my doubts. They didn't know the whole story, which went back to my childhood. Back in Pringles, when I was a child, the arrival of a magician was an event of the greatest importance for me and my friends. One, at least, came to our town to perform every year, always in the Spanish Theater, before a full house. All the children from our block would be there without fail, and we would spend weeks afterward analyzing the show, trying to decide, in heated discussions, how much deception and how much real magic there had been in each trick. But the thing was, I was nearsighted, and even with my glasses, I couldn't see well at a distance. The tricks that the Magician performed on that faraway, elevated stage depended entirely or almost entirely on precise details, which I could only have made out had I been standing within arm's reach. I was accustomed to deciphering and interpreting those blurry visions, and I understood more or less what was going on, but when my friends mentioned certain movements or gestures, or a small object used in a trick, I didn't know what they were talking about. I would rather have died than admit that I couldn't see properly, so I listened to their comments with the greatest attention, memorized them, reconstructed the Magician's performance clearly in my mind's eye according to what they had said, and there came a point where I was able to join in the discussion, as fully informed as the others.

These visual and mental gymnastics prepared me for a peculiar exercise in fabulation. I was the only one in the group who'd traveled to Buenos Aires, where my parents took me once or twice a year. And when I came back, I told my friends about the magic shows that I had seen (these were imaginary, of course; I was never taken to see a magician in Buenos Aires). One by one, I described for them the tricks that I had invented during the endless train rides. It wasn't as hard for me to invent them as it would have been for a prestidigitator, because I was inventing what the audience could see, without knowing how it was done (and whether it was sleight of hand or what—with the charming naivety of small-town kids in those days—we called "real magic"). Even so, it was quite a bit of work to make sure that the tricks were varied, interesting, plausible, and easy to visualize from an oral description. I enjoyed a considerable success, which went to my head, I suspect. When the time came to decide what I would be when I grew up, I chose to be a writer, and all I have done throughout my career is repeat the formula.

I left Francisco's store thinking that it might have been a mistake to consult my literary friends first, or at all. Ultimately, they could live without me, and I could live without them. I should have been looking to life, not letters, and in my case life had another name: marriage. But as it happened, my wife was away in Europe on a study-abroad program and wouldn't be back for a few weeks. We had been emailing each other every day, but so far I hadn't said anything about what had happened to me, although she was the first person I'd thought of. Now the time had come to tell her. But what would I say? I was far from having made up my mind and I knew that I would go on hesitating right up until the last moment: that indecision was what I should convey, to hear how she would react.

We couldn't actually talk, because of the time difference. So I would have to write to her. A strange weariness made me procrastinate. I had a whiskey, watched television, and went to bed early, having resolved to email her first thing in the morning. It didn't work out that way, because before sitting down at the computer, I realized that I would have to make myself very clear and comprehensible. In writing, I wouldn't be able to resort to gestures, tones of voice, and dramatic pauses, as I had with Ernesto and Francisco. The crucial thing in this case, in order for it all to make sense, was to ensure that what I wrote was taken seriously: no simple matter, I suspected, given my record. After some inner deliberation, I set to work on a draft.

The task, as I had feared, was difficult. Handling such slippery material would not have been easy for anyone, and I made it even harder for myself by trying to endow the draft with a Borges-like precision and at the same time a *sprezzatura* that would downplay the drama. But not too much: I had to deliver a certain dose of drama to make my wife understand that I wasn't treating the situation lightly. The rest of my days were at stake, after all, and hers as well to some degree, since my decision could suspend our life together for an indefinite period. And I didn't want to be too tactful: I felt my email should sound like a cry from the heart. The hardest thing was describing the feats that the Magician of Parque Rivadavia had performed to convince me of his powers (to keep it simple, I wasn't going to mention what Ernesto and Francisco had done). I realized that it was easy enough to tell her what had happened, but that was exactly what compromised the story's credibility. I had to call on all of my literary resources, including some that I hadn't even known I possessed until then. I filled the pages of my notebook with crossings-out, corrections, and rewriting, adding layer after layer to the palimpsest of my perfectionism.

It took hours. No. That's an understatement. It took all day. What happened was that at some point the process of writing took over, controlling me as I'd hoped to control it, and led me into the territory of Literature itself. As long as I wasn't actually writing, I could pretend to be nonchalant about the written word, as I had the previous afternoon, when talking with Francisco. But as soon as I picked up a pen, I couldn't imagine not writing. And the decision that I was facing concerned precisely this activity, so deeply rooted in my habits. It occurred to me that the pages I was filling with my scribbles, this rough draft that would have be typed out and sent, by mysterious digital means (mysterious to me at least), might be the last thing I would write. Pages composed on the threshold of a journey into the supernatural, where writing would be magically forbidden. Formulated like that, the subject seemed promising, and I couldn't resist sketching out its narrative possibilities in a couple of sentences, which soon became dozens ... It's not every day that you get the chance to write the last thing you'll ever write in your life. The marvelous appeared at the gold tip of my pen, where it multiplied and embellished itself. I couldn't stop; the more I wrote, the more ideas and images came to me.

At seven, I went out for my usual evening walk. I hadn't completed the draft, but I needed some exercise to clear my head; when I got back, with my thoughts refreshed, I would add the finishing touches. The sky had clouded over, hastening the approach of night. Suddenly, as I set off, it struck me how much I stood to lose by giving up my life of domestic routines. Until then I had always resisted change but chided myself for it. What was the point of having a life if not to swap it for another? And there had never been such a momentous reason for me to change my life.

Unseasonably, the leaves were falling from the trees and settling into yellow mats that were soft underfoot. My walking was cushioned; it was slightly disturbing. The last daylight was filtering through the gaps in the buildings under construction. The traffic had eased off by then and was being replaced by a wind that blew obliquely across the street for some incomprehensible reason. I started walking on autopilot, as I always do when I'm grappling with a problem. I followed my habitual route, oblivious to everything, lost in thought. Strangely, the problem of how to write a clear and communicative report so my wife would understand the predicament that I was facing had pushed the actual predicament into the background. I forced myself to bring it back into focus, because in the end it was my life at stake, not a piece of writing. The people from the shantytown were rummaging through the trash. There were so many poor people in the world. Did they too have supernatural powers, like Ernesto and Francisco, powers that they declined to use because of some abstruse intellectual scruple? I doubted it. Surely if they did they wouldn't be acting out that abject spectacle of misery. Or would they? What did I know? I who had always had everything and was perhaps about to embark on a quest that would give me even more? Much more than everything, because I would attain a higher level of possession ...

To combat these half-articulated thoughts, I drew on all the energy that, like a distant shore, surrounded my mental fatigue (while keeping a little in reserve for my nine o'clock sudoku). If the adventure that lay before me had any value it was as a means of dispossession, a form of mysticism. And yet I hadn't been able to stop vaguely imagining all the things I might possess (as Francisco and Ernesto had shown me) and I was ashamed of myself. But then I interrupted my moralizing to make at least a provisional list of the luxury items I would be able to procure by transforming pebbles and tacks. And I couldn't think of a single one. It was as if the Montblanc and the first-edition copy of *Nouvelles impressions d'Afrique* had exhausted my desires. This made me feel like a genuine wretch, partly because of my lack of imagination and partly because I was clinging to that lack. In a gesture that I felt was heroic, and

*41*

perhaps it was, I took the pen and the book from the pocket of my Packard overcoat and threw them into a dumpster. The homeless people would take them away, not realizing their true value, which no one could know better than I. There was also the little gold cube in my pocket. For a moment, I hesitated. Wouldn't it be better to keep it, not for its fiduciary value but as an amulet? I wondered, but only for a moment. I threw the cube away too. I felt unburdened, as if I had triumphed over myself, and before I knew it, I was back home.

I went on writing into the night, traveling to my imaginary Abyssinia, until I realized that it was late and I still hadn't completed a proper draft of that crucially important message to my wife. Because of the time difference between Buenos Aires and the old continent, I still had the whole night ahead of me in which to compose a good draft, in concise and cogent form. But it was time for my whiskey, and I knew from repeated experience that my mental sharpness would decline after that, and I would be in no condition to perform such a delicate task. It was ten o'clock: there was no time to lose. I decided to improvise, straight from the heart, to put myself in my wife's hands, and let her be the one to decide. I had more faith in the deep-seated wisdom of a married woman than in Hegel. And although I didn't have much faith in myself, I surrendered to destiny and switched on the computer. Imagine how annoyed I was to find that the connection wasn't working. It happens. It had happened to me often enough. "You are not connected to the internet," said the little sign on the screen. I have no understanding of these things. They make me feel completely helpless. It was an excellent excuse to do nothing and put it all off, as usual, until the next day, except that in this case there would be no next day. So I forced myself to act. I put my Packard overcoat back on, pocketed my notebook, and went out in search of an internet café.

Where would I find an internet café open at ten on a Saturday night? There, on the edge of the desert ... The dirty, winding streets were dimly lit, but the stars seemed to have descended; they were fluttering desperately. There was no moon, or it was hidden by one of the apartment buildings for workers, lined up in what appeared to be an endless procession. The lamps that illuminated this neighborhood so poorly were widely spaced; the light from one could barely reach the edge of the light from the next. Walking through a dim intermediate zone, I decided to check the silhouette of my deformed hand, to verify its true shape. Certain conditions are more clearly revealed by a silhouette than by three-dimensional sight. The opportunity was ideal, and my search for an internet café, which I suspected was doomed to fail, could be postponed for a minute or two.

I raised my left hand and moved it about in the penumbra until I found the optimal position. I couldn't recognize what I saw; perhaps the experiment was too radical. After so many dislocations and all the subsequent surgery, the shape of my hand had gradually changed. The slowness of the change (the dislocations didn't happen every day, two or three times a year at most), had given me time to adapt, and habit, as has often been remarked, can neutralize vision more effectively than blindness. This was confirmed for me by the silhouette of my hand, standing out against the faint luminosity like a paper cutout. Foreshortening made it resemble a clumsy octopus—that is, another monstrosity. A tentacle reached out and retracted in response to the cramps and tremors that had seized control of my poor, wounded hand. I was seeing it as a foreign object, a painful relic from my time in hospitals and operating rooms, a souvenir I was still carrying around, but only because it was attached to me. I lost myself in contemplation, to an accompaniment of scattered dissonances. The whole night became one great echo of silence. My posture must have attracted the attention of the Muslims. Experts in religious gymnastics, they probably thought I was summoning a demon or casting a spell. Their white robes fluttered as they crossed at the intersections. I was seeing them out of the corner of my eye, which gave them a ghostlike air. They emerged from one zone of shadow only to plunge into another. The stitched incisions crisscrossing my left hand seemed to be opening, thirstily. Perhaps the deformity of that hand, which made it absolutely unique, had given it exceptional powers. I should have been studying it properly, instead of wasting time on optical illusions. The way the muscles worked had changed, so my two hands functioned asymmetrically. The conventional balance had been upset, but perhaps there had been a gain elsewhere.

In the end, both hands went back in my pockets and I set off in a random direction, resuming the search for an unlikely internet café from which to send the message to my wife. Once again the streets offered me their aimless emptiness. It was as if I had been transported back into the past. And yet the quest for an internet café didn't seem too incongruous, because the cost of digital modernity had fallen to the point where it coexisted with poverty, that contemporary form of the past. I summoned my courage and plunged into the darkest, downward-leading alleyways. Perhaps, unconsciously, I didn't want to find what I was looking for, or send the message, or put my wife in the picture; it wouldn't have been the first time that a dense layer of resignation had prevented me from taking action. On this occasion, however, the very unlikeliness of success created a momentum that kept me going.

And I went so far that eventually, as a reward for my persistence, one of those twisting alleyways gave onto an enormous breadth of firmament. I stepped forward, dazzled by the blackness of the sky. The stars seemed interchangeable, like items in a collection. Since I was looking up, not ahead, I was bound to bump into the parapet, and I did. Then I worked out where I was, which—under the circumstances—meant shifting heavy spatiotemporal masses from one side of my brain to the other.

The Nile, which I had not seen until then, was flowing at my feet. The ripples, the shore and the whole landscape seemed to have been drawn in fine white lines on a black background. Lotuses were opening, breathing dewy vapor; jackals were cautiously coming down to drink, while the ibis stood still, their heads held high. A small, solitary hippopotamus emerged from the slime beside a deserted raft. The scene flickered in the darkness, appearing and disappearing, in negative ... It was all moving horizontally, with the current, but much more slowly. My contemplation was becoming unreal, paradoxically. Minutes earlier, I could have sworn that lotuses, ibis, and jackals belonged to the legendary realm of archaeology, or that they were put on show exclusively for gullible tourists. Yet there they were in front of me, placidly disposed in that midnight diorama. I was the sole witness. I wondered if it was always like that, if all the things whose real existence we tend to dismiss, out of habit or intuitive but unexamined conviction, really do exist, and exactly where we have been told that they are to be found.

But before I go on, I must explain something; otherwise this transition might seem like a mere literary flourish or a stunt to astound the reader.

This is what had happened. That previous Saturday, in Buenos Aires, when I'd found that internet café I was looking for and gone online, before sending that confounded message or confession to my wife, I looked at the new messages in my inbox and found one that completely changed my plans. It was an invitation, for the coming week, to a conference in Cairo. The organizers apologized profusely for the short notice, but I wasn't surprised; it was typical of them. They belonged to e-flux, a collective with which I had a special affinity; I had collaborated with them in the past. Their events were always set up at the last minute, and their overall informality was balanced by generous funding, provided by Scandinavian royalty. They must have been expecting me to say yes, because they had sent me the ticket, which I printed off in the café with the help of the Peruvian attendant. All I told my wife was that I would be going on a short trip; I left the serious content of the draft for later. Then I went home to pack, and the next morning, on the way to the airport, I stopped by Parque Rivadavia and left a message for the Magician with a stallholder I knew: something had come up, I needed another week, I was postponing our appointment to the following Sunday (same time, same place). Since he had no opportunity to reply, he couldn't say no.

Once in Egypt, I was so absorbed by the conference with its whirl of activities and obligations that the week flew past. And by the time I remembered, it was already Saturday. My flight was at midnight, but because of the time difference I would be able to keep my appointment, having considered my wife's response. The problem was that I still hadn't written to her. I packed my suitcase, and since there was no internet connection at the hotel, went out in search of an internet café.

The parallel between the two situations was so striking (in both, for the same reason, I was out searching for an internet café on a Saturday night), and what had happened in between was so irrelevant to the events related here, that I had the bright idea of simply skipping ahead, to keep my narration from getting bogged down. But that backfired, because I have had to insert here this tedious explanation. What can you do? If you want people to understand the story you're telling, you have to explain one thing after another.

Anyhow. Since I've already lost the advantage of speed, and the purity of narration advocated by Walter Benjamin, since I'm already sunk in the dense molasses of explanation, I can hold things up for a few more pages. Admittedly, I was exaggerating when I claimed that what had happened between the two situations was completely irrelevant to the substance of this story. The intellectual activity of that week in Cairo had effected a revolution in my thought, a change of ideas whose magnitude I still hadn't fully measured.

The theme of the conference was Contemporary Art. I had been granted the honor of delivering the opening address. I improvised, using notes that I had made during the flight. It wasn't hard because over the years I had done a lot of reading and thinking about the central theme of my talk, which was the way in which airport customs checks stop artists benefiting fully from the globalization of the events in which they participate. The checks are increasingly rigorous, and the instruments of detection have become implacable (they're even using dogs now, for God's sake), so artists, faced with the prospect of an unpleasant encounter with the police, give up the idea of traveling with

drugs, or simply give up traveling altogether. If they
don't travel, they are disadvantaged personally and ar-
tistically, since they are cut off from the cosmopolitan
scene and contact with their peers: it's a mutilation of
their experience. And if they do travel with drugs—a
hypothetical case, since none of them dare—they are
risking serious mental trauma. There were two aspects
to my critique—institutional and personal—and they
were closely related. On the personal level, creativity
itself is at risk. Artificially induced states of mind are
the drivers of creation; without them artists would be
reduced to elaborating their real experiences, which
would confine them to the tradition, if not to pathetic
psychodrama. The mechanisms of institutional repres-
sion restrict them to a national scene and, even within
the nation, to overland travel, which is a waste of valu-
able time. Artists prevented from attending interna-
tional events are at a disadvantage with respect to their
colleagues. But since they are all in the same situation,
the disadvantage is generalized, and contemporary art
is drained of its substance. This is what explains the
proliferation of geographically dispersed biennales:
travel turns back on itself and creativity ferments in its
birthplace. Taken to its logical conclusion, this process
would cover the planet with fixed points, and the work
of art would attain its definitive contemporaneity by
virtue of its specific spatiotemporal location.

As I had foreseen, my thesis provoked a heated con-
troversy, which was not limited to my speech but spilled
over into all the other sessions. Two distinct kinds of

objections were raised: first, it could be argued that drugs can be found everywhere, so traveling artists should be able to count on the good will of their local peers and hosts to obtain what they need, wherever they happen to be. This objection can easily be refuted by appealing to specific needs. The drug that activates artistic creation is the product of a time and a place, to the point where it actually takes the form of the time and place in which it was produced. Does that mean that drugs are merely a metaphor? Quite the contrary: they are what metaphors are made of.

The second kind of objection was based on the electronic flow of information, which enables virtual travel: it might not be quite as good as the real thing, but it comes pretty close and is much less inconvenient. At this point the argument became more complicated and subtle, turning back on itself: the ghostliness of a mass of heterogeneous data could be an inverted figure for drugs-as-metaphor. But who wants to get high on metaphors?

The interest I had aroused, which had prompted this debate with myself and its various ramifications, distracted me completely from the greater predicament that I was in, and just as I had done the previous week, I kept putting off the writing and the sending of the message to my wife. When I went to the hotel's business center at the last minute, on Saturday night, just before setting off for the airport, I was surprised to find that the computers had lost their internet connection, and I had to go out and look for an internet café. Even then, my mind was elsewhere. As well as affording me the gratification of causing a stir, the conference had allowed me to see my literary activity in a new light. For the first time, I was seriously wondering if my real talent was not for fiction but for theory, criticism, or the philosophical essay. And I found myself asking why, as an adolescent, I had decided impulsively, and without any serious reflection, that I would write novels. What if that had been a mistake, a huge mistake that sent my whole career in the wrong direction? The fact that my novels had found readers, and even admirers, proved nothing. Only I knew what was right for me. I wondered if it wouldn't be possible to take all my novels, extract the ideas, and rewrite them as treatises, to eliminate all the fiction by a process analogous to chemical dissolution—by means of an acid, for example—and I found this project more and more convincing; it came to seem predestined and irresistible. It was as if that imaginary acid were already acting on my brain, revealing the invention of stories as a childish, almost ridiculous activity, not to mention all the work of making them plausible by providing circumstantial details, and creating characters and atmospheres ...

Nevertheless, I was not unaware that I may have been deceiving myself, swayed by one of the passing enthusiasms that have played a large part in my intellectual biography. I needed another opinion, from someone levelheaded and objective, and who better than my wife? That Saturday night, as I wandered through the dark Egyptian streets in search of an internet café, I had not decided which of my two dilemmas to consult her about. And I had to choose, because they were mutually exclusive.

My thoughts kept splitting. I had a lot to think about but I've never been able to focus my thinking on one thing for long, and the circumstances were making it especially difficult. When people dug a grave in Egypt, they would find the place taken, occupied by a corpse. There was no point looking for somewhere more remote, or digging into solid rock, or the basement of one's house. And since the dead could not be buried, they ended up as crocodile food: they were given to those horrible armored saurians for breakfast, in the sinister dawns of the delta. The females, sore from monstrous couplings, bellies bulging with eggs, opened deep trenches in the holy mud. The sun came out, red as fire, a steely sky closed over that world of contrasts. The terrified inhabitants of the land took refuge in the mastabas built by their ancestors, which often collapsed due to overcrowding. All this must have been normal for the Egyptians, but for me it was new and strange. It was like one of those scenes that I had been so fond of inventing in my former life as a novelist (I was already thinking of writing as a thing of the past). I had spent the week in the refrigerated rooms of the museum, utterly oblivious to these legendary realities. The conference papers and their intellectual games had eclipsed the devouring of the recently deceased that was taking place just a short walk away. Everything was happening at once, except at one moment in the daily cycle: midnight, when all the simultaneities came undone. And midnight was approaching. That was the time when I was supposed to be at the airport to catch my plane. I was sad to be leaving such a picturesque place. You can't get to know Egypt in a week. There were so many things I hadn't seen. But I was also keen to get home. I would be returning with fascinating scenes imprinted on my retinas; interpreting them would take many years, perhaps the rest of my life. Of course, in that time I would travel again, to places with as many intriguing attractions, or even more, and the work of decoding the new images from the register of memory would begin while the old ones were still being processed.

Everything was interrelated, or rather, everything was coming together, converging on a precipitous vertex, like an imperialist perspective: the sham magic that my novels had staged, and the real magic opening up before me. But also my possible conversion from novelist to essayist, and third, and most important, my going on as a writer or giving up. Nothing was decided; the alternatives formed parallel lines, appearing to converge but never touching.

Meanwhile, I had continued to walk along the esplanade beside the Nile. A figure was coming toward me, emerging from a patch of darkness into the splendid moonlight. It was the fat guy from Parque Rivadavia: Ovando, the Famous Magician. He was coming for me, for my brain. I wasn't too surprised to see him there. I could almost say that I had been expecting him. Nor was I amazed, as perhaps he had hoped I would be, that he had come flying over the Atlantic, among the clouds and stars, like a self-propelled meteorite. Hadn't I done the same thing, sitting comfortably in the plane, reading a good book? Which was better? And hadn't he come after me, following in my wake? As a result of recent events, Magic had begun to lose its magic in my eyes.

To tell the truth, there was also a more concrete reason for my lack of surprise: I had seen him repeatedly in other foreign metropolises, in Madrid, Paris, Istanbul, San Francisco ... so often that the sight of him no longer took me aback; I had almost come to expect it. And I would simply avoid him; I didn't want him bothering me on the Acropolis or in the Latin Quarter as he did every Sunday in Parque Rivadavia. I suppose I must have wondered, in a vague and idle way, where he got the money for traveling around the world like that. Now I understood, but only because he had revealed his plan. As he approached me, I got in first and told him that I still hadn't made up my mind. New objections had occurred to me. There was the question of age. I didn't want to be like all those people who put off enjoying life until they come into an inheritance; by the time they get the money, their youth is gone and they want to live every minute, every second to the full, so they pursue experience with a pathetic avidity. For me to receive the gift of Magic at my age would have been rather like that, and I lacked the spiritual resources to handle it.

He didn't give me time to present my arguments, which might have been just as well, because if I had started speaking more and more ideas would have occurred to me, and I would no doubt have got myself into an inextricable tangle.

"It's too late."

"What do you mean? Didn't we agree that on Sunday …?"

He didn't bother to reply. The time for words had come to an end. I felt a deep despondency, foreshadowing a resignation that would root me to the spot. He had been transfigured. His beard, which was thicker than ever, gleamed in the light reflected off the water. Now we were walking toward a circular pavilion, which gave the impression of being too close, like an architectural model. A cloud obscured the moon, and the Magician took me by the arm, affirming his dominion. What had happened to me? In the course of my life I had often known periods of discouragement and apathy, and felt that my career as a writer was coming to an end. The feeling had always grown little by little, but there, in the Egyptian night, it had sprung upon me suddenly, without warning. Something was sucking my energy away.

The construction into which he led me was made up of disused mastabas built one over the other. It was vast, almost like a city, beneath a dome of stone. The entranceways were askew, the inside black as soot. Little animals scurried away in the darkness (they had not been *born* small, it occurred to me, but had been shrunk down to that size by a procedure of some kind).

He had me where he wanted me—in the realm of

Magic, but Magic as Death. This, I thought, could serve as my farewell to the magical, which had been so bad for my writing. It was an old error, the original error, I might even say, staining all that I had done.

That didn't matter anymore. What should have mattered was the future. I could see it as if through a veil: the real world, the world of work, of study, of abilities. A panorama of results, triumphs of will and knowledge. Strangely, it resembled Nature. Not this humid darkness full of jackals, but living light in the open air, birds hopping from branch to branch in monumental trees, plummeting from the heights like masses obeying the law of gravity, or rising to the very tops with barely a flap, propelled by the invisible springs that also produced the tireless chirping in their tiny throats. And behind that tracery, there were forests, mountains, and lakes, against the ever-blue background of sky hung above and all around the sea.

But let us return to the prosaic reality of what happened. Ovando had brought me to the exact place where my brain would emit the waves that, in combination with his magical skills, would empower him to achieve world domination, his long-cherished dream as a failed writer. At last I had fathomed his plan and understood his motives. He had fed me a tall tale, and in my naivety, I had swallowed it. But he had lied to me with the truth. He had led me by the nose with a baggy plot full of this and that, almost a pastiche of the novels I had written in my Pierre Loti phase. Once he had what he was after, he would dig a grave and find my corpse in it, waiting there ever since I'd written my first book, forty years earlier. That way, no one could accuse him of murder.

The operation began with deep and terrifying reverberations. My brain was a hundred-thousand-megatron engine. Small, flat, phosphorescent figures streamed out of the Magician's mouth and were deflected by the waves that had suddenly begun to radiate from my brain; they were caught up in the concentric expansion like plastic pegs on a clothes line. Unable to bear the aesthetic of those configurations, I shut my eyes. But I could still feel the pulsing, and it was growing stronger.

That was when my B-grade-horror Svengali betrayed his stupidity. He had made a common mistake (I had made it myself more than once): he had put his trust in the quality of an idea and set about implementing it without having done the relevant calculations. He can't have had much of a head for figures. The power of my personal radiation overcame the resistance of the Universe, which began to shudder dangerously. This should not have bothered me, given how close I was to death. But the problem was that we were inside an old ruin, and by the time we realized it—both at once—it was too late. The collapse had begun.

Stunned, the Magician shut his mouth, and the little figures that had come out of it disintegrated along with my mind waves. When the artificial illumination produced by the phosphorescence failed, I realized that it had made the inside of the building look like a darkroom. It had been the sort of light that doesn't affect wet negatives. The figures were replaced by the blunt three-dimensionality of stone blocks crashing down, each weighing hundreds of tons. We had to get out of there as soon as we could. Horizontal and vertical quake alarms sounded uselessly. All of a sudden, Ovando's power over me evaporated, as if a button had been pressed. My mind was recovering its (relative) autonomy, but what use was it to me now? The first pile of fallen stones had blocked the exit. My hope that the rocking of the masonry would stop along with my cerebral radiation was short-lived. The underpinning of that ancient edifice had been damaged beyond repair, and only one outcome was possible: total demolition, with the two of us inside.

A huge slab fell straight down and landed just inches from where we were standing. Moonlight shone in through the gap that it had left overhead. When the cloud of dust began to settle, I saw the Magician running around in a panic, having abandoned all semblance of dignity: it was "every man for himself" now. Apparently, his powers deserted him as soon as a serious problem arose. Another block fell and made the ground shake. The Magician swayed like a balloon full of hydrogen, and spun like a top with his arms held high and a look of abject terror on his face. And that was the last I saw of him; he was hidden by the dust and darkness, and the masses of falling stone. The whole structure was about to collapse. I prepared myself to die. I can't pretend that I managed this with Socratic philosophical calm, but the paralyzing effects of terror made it look that way.

I tipped my head back, not to see the firmament and bid farewell to the stars; it was more a nervous reflex. A silhouette stood out against the sky's illuminated black, on the edge of the building's roof, and I knew who it was immediately, although it was the last person I was expecting to see: my wife. In the first moment of confusion, I thought that in some parallel world I had found the internet café and finally been able to send her the long-delayed message. But no, I hadn't, and if I had, the response would have been an email, not her instantaneous appearance in Egypt. Whatever had happened, this was no time for speculation: the collapse was accelerating with each passing second. I tried to cry out, but all that emerged from my dry, dusty throat was a pathetic croak. "She'll see me die," I thought, "and her tears will dampen the heap of rough tombstones." But I soon realized that there was no reason to be so pessimistic: she had come equipped with a rope ladder, which dropped unfurling down to me. I grabbed it and began to climb, ignoring the multiple pains resulting from my history of dislocations. Around me, stone blocks the size of one-room apartments were hurtling past in a veritable barrage. I was rising while all around me fell, which gave a false impression of speed. When I reached the top I was at the level from which I had begun, because the whole building had come down. But we were safe. We ran away.

"I thought you were in Heidelberg," I said.

"Well, you were wrong, as you can see. I've been following you from the start. I didn't let you out of my sight, not that I doubt your ability to get out of a scrape, most of the time anyway, but when the scrape is a product of your imagination, it can turn against you, I mean it can turn into something real, although you never meant for it to escape from the realm of your thoughts, and that's where I have to step in."